GEORGE MACKAY BROWN was born in Stromness, where his home has always been. He studied for a year at Newbattle Abbey College when Edwin Muir was its Warden, and gained a degree in English from Edinburgh University. After two further years at the university he returned to Orkney, in 1964. Since then he has earned his living as a writer. He has been awarded the O.B.E., three honorary degrees and several prizes, including the James Tait Black Memorial Prize for *The Golden Bird: Two Orkney Stories*.

GUNNIE MOBERG was born in Sweden. She came to Edinburgh to study art and settled in Orkney in 1976. A freelance photographer, she has illustrated several books including *Stone*, a sequence of poems by George Mackay Brown, and *The Orkney Story* by Liv Schei. Her husband runs a bookshop, Stromness Books and Prints.

ERLEND BROWN, nephew of George Mackay Brown, has always lived in Stromness. He studied painting at the Edinburgh College of Art. His paintings and drawings have been shown at exhibitions all over Scotland and in Norway and Switzerland. He is Curator of the Pier Arts Centre, Stromness.

John Murray

# Portrait of Orkney

GEORGE MACKAY BROWN

*Photographs by* Gunnie Moberg

*Drawings by* Erlend Brown

First published 1981
This edition first published 1988
by John Murray (Publishers) Ltd
50 Albemarle Street, London W1X 4BD

Text © George Mackay Brown 1981, 1988
Photographs © Gunnie Moberg 1988
Drawings © Erlend Brown 1988

Brown, George Mackay, 1929
Portrait of Orkney
I. Scotland. Orkney – 1979
i. Title
ii. Moberg, Gunnie
iii. Brown, Erlend
941.1,32

ISBN 0–7195–4539–0
Printed and bound in Great Britain by
Butler & Tanner Ltd, Frome and London

The publishers and the author acknowledge permission to reproduce copyright material as follows: Extract from *The Man on my Back* by Eric Linklater, reprinted by permission of A. D. Peters; 'Childhood' from *Collected Poems* by Edwin Muir, reprinted by permission of Faber & Faber and of Oxford University Press, Inc., New York; 'Celestial Kinsmen' from *Orkney Variants and Other Poems* by Robert Rendall, reprinted by permission of Mr R. P. Rendall.

ALSO BY GEORGE MACKAY BROWN

*Poems*
Loaves and Fishes, The Year of the Whale, Fishermen with Ploughs,
Winterfold, Selected Poems, Voyages

*Short stories*
A Calendar of Love, A Time to Keep, Hawkfall,
The Sun's Net, Andrina, The Golden Bird

*Plays*
A Spell for Green Corn
Three Plays: The Well, The Loom of Light,
The Voyage of St Brandon

*Novels*
Greenvoe, Magnus, Time in a Red Coat

*Essays*
An Orkney Tapestry, Letters from Hamnavoe,
Under Brinkie's Brae

*For children*
The Two Fiddlers, Pictures in the Cave,
Six Lives of Fankle the Cat

*In Memoriam*
Edwin and Willa Muir

# Contents

―――

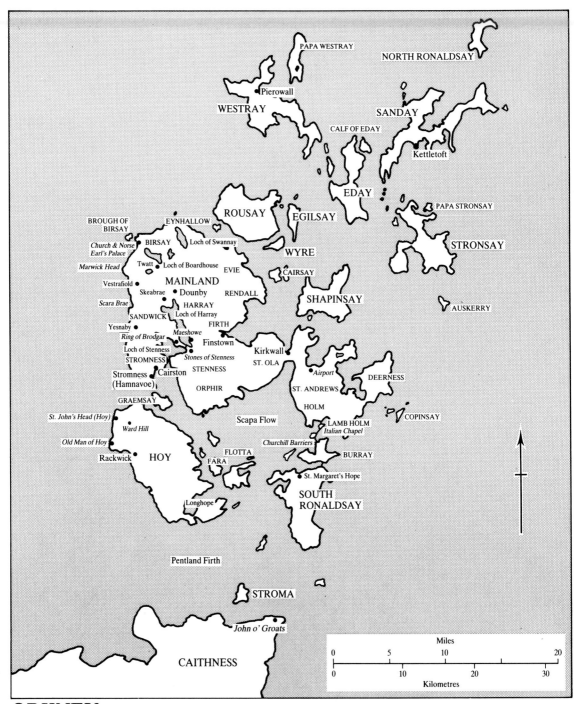

# ORKNEY

# I
# *People*
====

The people of Orkney today are a mingled weave. Over the winter fires, when we are not watching television, some of us like to think of ourselves as 'sons of the Vikings'. To go into the history of these medieval pirates and reivers is not such an edifying experience. No doubt the Norsemen who settled in the islands, and farmed and traded and fished, form an important strain in the modern Orcadian. Especially in the North Isles, you can see tall fair-haired blue-eyed men and women who seem to be 'typically Scandinavian'.

But our modern blood springs from many sources. What ingenious folk built the brochs? Who were the Picts? *Orkneyinga Saga* is silent about them – you might think the sagamen would have delighted in telling how the first Norsemen outwitted and destroyed the Picts, and made of their keeps wide strewments of stone. But there is nothing. Perhaps what happened is that there was slow infiltration from the east over centuries – a storm-driven longship, gaunt-faced traders, silent night-shrouded raiders, even a tentative settler in this island and that – until in the end the new culture, laws, ways of sailing and farming took over completely. If that was the way of it, there is probably as much Pictish blood in us as Norse. Even if the conquest was sudden and violent, we may be sure that the girls were not despised.

*The blond word-man in the first death-ship said, 'We removed stone from stone, on a western beach.' Sigurd the skipper said, 'I think we can build a hall and a few proper farms here...' Sigurd said later, 'Take the best of the women down to the ship...'*

The sources go much further back. No doubt, such are the blood's intricate interweavings, some of our remote ancestors were at the building of Brodgar

'They dragged the huge stones from Vestrafiold and trundled them all the way to the dark moor between the lochs. They manhandled monoliths for the master-masons of Maeshowe.'

and Skara Brae. They dragged the huge stones from Vestrafiold and trundled them all the way to the dark moor between the lochs. They manhandled monoliths for the master-masons of Maeshowe. What kind of people they were – their laws and music and language – are utterly lost. But it seems they saw life not as a brief line, birth-to-death, but as a circle which has neither beginning nor end.

### The New Chief: Quanterness

*First was given, with new edges,*
*A breast cut*
*Deep, for a welling of light.*

*The moon-thirled women*
*Turned wheels*
*All about him: wool, milk, stone.*

*The chief came, hooded,*
*To a red stone marked OX. Thereafter*
*Furrow and fire were ours.*

*(Who chose this man? Roots*
*Cried, stars sang,*
*Gulls wrote a name in the air and in water.)*

*Yesterday he idled*
*Grass-biting, a herdboy. Now*
*He rules, horned, from the centre.*

*As we are drawn*
*To snow and eclipse, his hand*
*Makes the sign of the sun.*

*He died one shearing time,*
*Webs of winter on him.*
*He returns, lissom, a boy again, with leaf and lamb.*

Were there other more mysterious ancestors still, shadows upon darkness? For them, primitive and short-lived as they were, the land and sea, after the retreat of the ice, must have seemed a new marvellous place, swarming with plants and animals and birds and fish that were more their kin than their prey (though, to live, they were forced to hunt them).

But finally and irrefutably, it was the Norse laws and culture that triumphed. Because they were masterly story-tellers, and delighted in that art in all its purity, we have in *Orkneyinga Saga* a matchless record of the way their earls and great men and women lived and thought. They delighted too in the intricate web of kinship; some of the sagas begin with a long formal account, going many generations back, of what lineage the chief characters in the story to be told were begotten. This gift has come down in all its essentials to certain modern Orkney men and women; you have simply to name a person in the presence of these 'kin-redders', and they will immediately surround that name with cousins, step-brothers, uncles, grandfathers: the web, fixed deep in time, may span the world nowadays from Vancouver to New South Wales. If it sounds like a dry art, there are in every family certain incidents and involvements to give it spice.

The Norsemen had hardly taken over when, naturally, their chiefs were drawn into the orbits of Scottish high society. Whether we like it or not, the greatest of the Orkney earls, Thorfinn the Mighty, was a cousin of King Macbeth of Scotland. Thorfinn did not look at all like 'a son of the Vikings':

*He was of all men the tallest and strongest; he was ugly; he had black hair, a large nose and a rather dark complexion. He had enormous energy, and he desired above all things riches and good fame...* Orkneyinga Saga

The Scottish influence grew over the generations; it was natural, Norway was far away eastward, and the growing kingdom of Scotland lay just across the Pentland Firth. Yet the language of the Norsemen was such a vivid inheritance to this increasingly mingled race that it was remembered here and there, in croft and noust, until late in the eighteenth century. There was a sufficient scattering of the old words only fifty years ago for Dr Hugh Marwick to put together a dictionary of them, *The Orkney Norn*.

What the *Saga* does not tell us is what life was like for the common people of Orkney and Shetland between the eighth and thirteenth centuries. There is one glimpse only, among heroic battle shouts, intrigues, burnings, festive songs in the high hall; that is the moving story of how Earl Rognvald fished dangerous waters with a Shetland crofter, and how afterwards the shore women laughed as their hooded lord slipped and fell in the seaweed. . .

But there they lived and drudged, generation after generation, in their little 'toonships' beside the sea, or on the loch-shore, breaking the soil with primitive shares, the men berated by their women (the women of the north have seemed to be always more powerful characters than any other women in the world), reaping the sudden silver harvest and the slow golden harvest, hedged in by dark supernatural powers, hoarding a bit of butter and a few dried fish to pay the earl or the bishop his rent.

> *I rent and till a patch of dirt*
> *Not much bigger than my coat.*
> *I keep a cow and twelve swine*
> *And some sheep and a boat.*
> > *Drudgings, stone.*
>
> *The name of my wife is Hild.*
> *Hild has a bitter tongue.*
> *She makes passable butter and ale.*
> *Her mouth brims and brims with bairnsong.*
> > *Driftings, stone.*
>
> *What's winter? A thousand stars,*
> *Shrinkings of snow, an empty pail.*
> *All summer I go, a drenched ox*
> *Between the plough and the flail.*
> > *Drudgings, stone. . .*

Yet the drudgery and the drift were brightly starred with festivals and junketings: Yule, Beltane, Johnsmas, Lammas, Hallowe'en, Saints' days. And such natural events as birth, marriage, death were not allowed to pass into oblivion without music, ale, dancing feet. To see an ancient Orkney wedding must have been an entrancing experience: the long column of countryfolk, led by a fiddler, wending its way two by two between the bride's house and the minister's manse, and back again after the ceremony, that one white splash among the sombre homespun. Then, in the barn, the drinking and mirth and dancing went on till beyond cockcrow. Before the revellers went home they

'The long column of country folk, led by a fiddler, wending its
way two by two...' (Photo taken during filming of *The Privilege*,
based on a story by George Mackay Brown)

drank, in a sunwise circle, from the bride's cog – a round wooden vessel filled with hot ale, spices, whisky... Often the wedding celebrations went on for days, as if these folk were reluctant (and who shall blame them?) to return once more to the uncertain wheel of agriculture.

### Bride Song

*In the barn, fiddle and flute*
*Are at odds, the dancing feet*
*Slower and heavier stamp,*
*The ale sinks low in the jar.*
*I unlatch a secret door.*
*'Come quickly. I've turned the cold sheet.*
*I have put*
*Only a little oil in the lamp.'*

They were so humble and anonymous that originally they had only the names given them in baptism, and if it was necessary to particularise some person more closely, they called him or her 'Peter's son' or 'Magnus's dottor', or 'Thorfinn's son'. So the surnames changed with every generation: to a hunter of genealogies it is impossibly confusing. There must be records of a fairly definite time when everyone, possibly in order that the earl might have a more precise roll-call of the governed (for fiscal or other reasons), was compelled to take a fixed surname. The Orcadians solved the situation simply: they called themselves by the district or parish or island where they lived at the time – Marwick, Linklater, Halcrow, Heddle, Firth, Harra, Corston, Corrigall, Cursiter, Rendall, Baikie, Isbister, Twatt... (Some argue that these names were given to families who had removed to another island or parish.) It is possible to argue that Orcadians with these 'district names' are older truer islanders than certain other families like Spence, Sinclair, Sutherland, Brown, Muir, Tait, who must have drifted in (from Scotland mainly) over the generations; it is probable that the infamous Stuart earls, so artistically sensitive but such bad governors, brought retinues of Scotsmen north with them into the islands. But the whole question of genealogy is such a tangle that it is foolish to say or conjecture how much native blood flows in a man's veins; and, as we've seen,

Orkney blood was from the beginning a sampling and a mixing from many wells.

It is arguably good for a people that they have variety in their ancestry. Most of us have seen what horrors were loosed on the earth only a few decades ago in the name of racial purity. Royal and noble families who tried, in past centuries, to maintain their blood untainted, had to endure for such folly incurable ailments of body and mind.

No doubt, in certain isolated parts of Orkney there was inbreeding that resulted in similar weaknesses. In the eighteenth century and earlier, it's said, a 'toonship' or a district resented it if a young man from another place came courting there; everything was done to discourage the suitor.

But one constant in Orkney history is the infusion of new blood, from this distant airt and that. Shipwrecks were common in former times. Did one of the Armada ships blunder against an Orkney coast? There are traditions of shipwrecked sailors from other lands, staying on and marrying local girls. There is the very moving story of a ship – either she was called 'Archangel' or she was out of that port – bound from Russia to America (loaded with immigrants, possibly) going ashore on Westray. Only one child, an anonymous boy, was saved from the wreck. That is why there was a family called Angel in Westray until recently.

When the Orkneymen, like their Norse forbears, sailed north-west in the nineteenth century after whales, or to work at the Hudson's Bay Company's fur posts, they did not remain celibate. Many of them loved their Indian wives well enough to take them back home, once they had earned enough money to rent a croft or a little farm in the islands.

The two world wars saw huge influxes of soldiers, sailors, airmen from all over Britain; and, as the war went on, from further afield. To an already complex bloodstream were added these exotic strains. No one shall say that the Orkney people were soiled or spoiled by the admixture. Indeed, one of the very gratifying things about young Orkney folk, however descended, is the perennial love they have for the islands. Many of them are forced of necessity to make their livings elsewhere; whenever an opportunity comes, they are true as salmon to the native streams. Is there a typical Orkney face? There are farmers and their wives at the Dounby Agricultural Show with apple-cheeks and ready laughter and shy careful speech. There are the fair-haired blue-eyed laconic

'Is there a typical Orkney face?' Perhaps young Elisabeth
from Evie?

fishermen from the islands. Islanders who do not belong to Kirkwall see in the faces of the capital lineaments not discernible in the outlying parishes and islands: an alertness (for want of a better word) springing perhaps from centuries of commercialism and close-knittedness. Stromnessians, too, are said to have their own speech and cast of countenance. 'The Orkney face' contains within itself great variety. All that can be safely said is that the earth and skies and sea that people live among get worked at last into the flesh and bone.

> *Many masks merge in an island face,*
> *Pict, Norseman, Scot,*
> *Salt wanderers, tremulous first-comers*
> *After the ice broke.*
> *Face of the countryman, strength of loam in it.*
> *Faces of fishermen, sailor : the eyes*
> *Level as horizons.*

There was a minister in Kirkwall in the late seventeenth century who wrote an enchanting book about the islands and their people. The English language was so rich then that merely to put pen to paper, it seems, begot felicities and delights. (We tend, increasingly, to speak and write more like computers than like imaginative beings.) Rev James Wallace, unlike the Cromwellian soldier who a few years earlier wrote a filthy ill-natured poem about Orkney and Orcadians, had a sweet nature and a perceptive eye. What he wrote about the islanders of three centuries ago is largely true today. Whether he was an Orkneyman or not, there is no doubt, judging from his beautiful prose, that he was under the spell of the islands. I can do no better than to make a little anthology of his remarks.

*The People here are generally Civil, sagacious, Circumspect, and Piously Inclined. Though Boethius reports them to be great Drunkards. . . Yet now it is not soo: For though they use strong Ale and Beer (the nature of the Climate requiring strong Liquor) yet generally they are sober, and Temperate, but withal much given to Hospitality and Feasting, very Civil and Liberal in their Entertaining of Strangers . . .*

The People are generally personable and Comelie. . . The Women are Lovely, and of a Beautiful Countenance, and are very Broodie and apt for Generation, One *Marjorie Bimbister* in the Parish of *Evie*, was in the year 1683 brought to bed of a Male Child, in the sixtie-third year of her Age...

By reason of the Temperance of their Dyet, and wholesomeness of the Air, the People usually Live to a good Age. A Man in the parish of *Ham*, died not many years since, who had Lived upwards of four-score years with his Wife in a Married estate. There is also a Gentleman yet living in *Stronsa*, who was begotten of his Father when he was a hundred years of age, and did live till he saw this same man's Children.

All speak English, with a good Accent, only some of the common People among themselves speak *Norse* or the old *Gottish Language*, which they have derived to them, either from the *Pights*, who first Peopled this Countrey, or from the *Danes* and *Norvegians*, in whose possession it once was.

# 2
## *A childhood*

═══

*Cull-ya! Cull-ya! Cull-ya!* cried the gulls at the end of the pier, especially when the wives were gutting their fish at the slipways and swilling them in the sea. *Cull-ya! Cull-ya!* – and white flashing wings.

Whitemaas we called them, or cull-yas. 'The cull-yas are crying for rain,' my mother would say, when for no reason the gulls would raise an outcry.

A fisherman sat on the pier, baiting his lines or mending his lobster-creels, when he wasn't fishing.

The fishermen went out in their white motor-boats, out through the rasping ropes of the Hoy Sound tiderace, out beyond Hoy or north as far as Birsay. When they returned with their baskets of haddock or cod, they emptied the fish into hand barrows and sold them along the street, weighing them on brass scales in front of the women who were waiting at the end of every close with their basins – sixpence a pound. 'And,' said one fisherman, 'there were fine outcries when we raised the price from threepence a pound!'

From the stone doorstep where I seemed to pass much of my early childhood, I could see most of the people who passed on the flagstone street above. There were the old shawled women going with purses and baskets for their errands.

*Thump-thump-thump!* – Two masons were always working on the street, replacing worn or broken flagstones. They thumped the new dressed flagstones in with enormous mallets requiring two hands.

*Clang-clang-clang!* – The town crier was on his rounds. Bronze swirlings of sound: then he would announce the arrival, for the coal merchant, of a cargo of 'best English coal', or an auction sale, or a concert in the Town Hall. Then he puffed out his cheeks and passed on to the next open space in the one long winding street of Stromness – and the boys scattered like starlings before him – because he did not seem to like boys, and would take a swipe at them with his stick.

The town fathers – nearly all business men or retired skippers – passed by in a group, making occasionally a solemn or portentous remark. On they went, having their morning constitutional, very important men.

*Honk-honk*! – Maybe twice a day a motor-car drove through the street. Only a few townsfolk had a motor-car – maybe the doctor or the hotelier.

Big boys could play football along the street, except when – oh horror! – the small rubber ball smashed a window of house or shop, and the irate tenant stood at the door, shouting and shaking a fist.

The two tall policemen gave no warning. Regularly – once an hour maybe – they proceeded south along the street, then north again. The boys who had been kicking a ball, or knocking on doors out of devilment, or stealing gooseberries from gardens, ran this way and that from the two tall policemen; up closes, down piers.

Another black figure: the minister. A respectful silence attended his passing. (Actually there were three ministers – four, counting the 'pisky' (episcopalian) – besides two Salvation Army officers, the Plymouth Brethren, Pentecostals, and itinerant evangelists. Stromness was a very religious town in the nineteen-twenties.)

Never a shout of *Time*! or *Drink up now, please*! Stromness, which had had in the 1830s about thirty-six places for the sale of drink, now had none. Not one tavern. Not a shebeen. Not an inn. The town had voted itself 'dry' after the First World War. The rowdy jovial interiors were shuttered. Put it down to the wild whaling men of the nineteenth century. Put it down to the Irish navvies of 1914–18, and the English marines, and the local weekend roisterers, rioters, and bruisers. The women and the temperance folk had had enough. Now the fishermen had to take bus eight miles to the 'Pomona' in Finstown or the 'Smithfield' in Dounby to wash the salt out of their throats. Now there was no 'White Horse' or 'Billy Clouston's' for the farmers, on a Wednesday afternoon, to seal their bargains with a dram.

Laughter, shouts, screams, thud of hundreds of feet ... The 'scholars' were out of school for their 11.15 a.m. play-time. They spent their ha'pennies on toffee and hot bakehouse buns.

*Clippety-clop*! *Clippety-clop*! – and the ringing of cans. The milkmen were on their rounds from a dozen farms near and far. No milk bottles, no cartons. The careful red-faced farmers poured the milk out of their great metal containers into the jugs and bowls on every doorstep: twopence a pint.

A few eccentric people mumbled and whirled past. There was one man who thought he was a ship.

Inside, my mother sang about her housework. Always she sang, not melodiously, but it was a happy contented sound; happy as a bee scrubbing at the washtub or stirring the stewpot, all day long.

Ah! the school bell had summoned the scholars back to the halls of learning that stood half-way up Brinkie's Brae, the hill that guards Stromness from the west. Ah, it was a bit lonely sitting on my doorstep with birds and a cat. I would cross the street and see what they were doing in the tailor shop. In the tailor shop Peter Esson and Willie Esson and my father sat at the bench, among spools of thread, triangular bits of chalk, lumps of resin, heavy iron geese, a pressing board, hundreds of cloth clippings, making trousers, skirts, and jackets. Sometimes the sewing machine would give a little burst of chatter. They eyed me solemnly. What day was it? Friday. My father reached into his pocket and gave me a ha'penny, 'my pension'. 'See you don't spend it all in one shop' . . . Lucky bags, liquorice, scotch mixture, black-striped balls, brandy balls, butternuts, bon-bons, pandrops, all-sorts: how could one choose among such treasures?

One day I looked up from my doorstep and a tinker stood there with a pack on her back. I dreamed, later, I was in a tinker's cart, and we were travelling on a narrow country road, up hill and down hill, for ever and ever.

*Hoo*! *Hoo*! – A double siren blast. The mail boat was coming into the harbour in the late afternoon, from Scrabster in Scotland, across the Pentland Firth. *Thud-thud-thud*! went the heart of the *St Ola*; then stopped, as she glided, black swan, through the harbour. The little *St Ola* docked at the wooden jetty. Then my father put on his postman's cap and went down with another postman to wheel the mail bags to the Post Office. (My father was a postman as well as a tailor.)

Oh, solemnity, whispers, long faces – Someone had died. The funeral would pass by. My mother pulled down the blind. All the blinds and curtains along the street were drawn. The street was sightless for an hour. The hearse, a splendid black coach drawn by horses, went past, followed by the solemn mourners... A long last road. The kirkyard was two miles outside the town, right on the Atlantic verge, where had been a medieval monastery. The kirkyard, with all its fine stones and inscriptions, looked a beautiful place to me, whenever my father took us for a walk on a Sunday afternoon.

I am talking about a summer morning in Stromness. A four-year-old boy sits in a web of golden hours...

The days shorten. A few snowflakes fall. The lamp is lit in the late afternoon. We have our bannocks and cheese, pancakes and jam, and tea, by lamplight.

For days there can be heard no sounds from the street for the howling of an easterly storm about the chimneys. Don't open the door too wide – a flurry of snow whirls in – the flames rear and roar up the lum.

The lamplighter is abroad after sunset, and he touches every gas lamp along the street to brightness.

The house is an igloo of perfect security. My sister tells me stories of forsaken lovers and broken hearts. My mother sings her happy tuneless songs as she irons shirts. The kettle sings on the stove. The cat sings on the mat. The door opens. My father enters from the storm, streaming. A lantern is pinned to his coat lapel, so that he can read the addresses. He comes in, briefly, to take the snow out of his eyes, to trim the flame of his lantern. Then out again, into the howling night, with his bag of letters.

And at 8 o'clock the stone hot-water bottle is filled, and I lie in bed, and listen with joy as the storm howls and rages about the stone piers and the houses.

The snow has fallen all night – the storm has blown itself out. I open the door to a transfigured world, a white enchanted Stromness. All the roofs wear tilted white bonnets. The old wives shake their shawls, lamenting, 'Oh, what awful weather!' I walk, I sink above my boots in thrilling whiteness. All sounds are muted. The cat shakes a paw. The birds leave prints, hopping from crumb to crumb.

A scarf is wound round my neck, two or three times.

A silent town, Stromness – until the school's out at 4 o'clock. How pure and sweet the tumultuous voices sound across the snow. The rough boys kill each other with snowballs. The gentler boys, and the girls, build snowmen with buttons down the quilted coats, and bits of coal for eyes, and a cold pipe in the

Warbeth: 'The kirkyard, with all its fine stones and inscriptions,
looked a beautiful place to me ...'

mouth. Sledges get dragged out of attics, out of garden sheds, up and up on trudging feet drawn to the summit of Oglaby. Then down, two or three on a sledge, swift, urgent, helter-skelter, down the long steep narrow brae to the street; time after time, until their cheeks are like apples and their eyes like stars.

And the stars flashing like jewels in the early evening – all night long till the late dawn wells in the south-east, over Scapa Flow.

The moon hung like a Chinese lantern over the chimney pots.

At night every shop window is bright. Truly it is a magical place, Stromness. The grocer shop where I go with my mother smells of coffee, cloves, cheese, apples, oranges, raisins. The kind old grocer, with spectacles and white whiskers, puts a sweetie in my mouth. At the Pier Head the Salvationists blow their trumpets and rattle tambourines. Mysterious shadowy figures come and go on the street, and greet each other, and linger beside a lighted square.

Oh, joy of winter! Then, one winter day, a name gets dropped: *Santa Claus* . . .
'Pooh,' say the elders, 'he won't be for three weeks yet.'

The letters get written, to be in good time, and sent to the North Pole on an updraught of the chimney, all alight!

Ask for what you like, what you get is an apple and an orange, a penny, a book or a toy sailing boat or a game of ludo. We unfold the gifts with pure enchantment: under the decorations and the mistletoe, with a bottle of ginger wine on the table, and a little assortment of celluloid cards on the mantelpiece, and a goose at noon brought in new roasted from the baker's.

Then it is Hogmanay, and a few furtive townsmen stand at the dark Pier Head waiting for the bus from Kirkwall to draw up. It contains precious parcels – the whisky and the beer they can no longer buy in Stromness; that once, in Hudson's Bay days, in whaling days, in the days of the herring fleets, seemed (to some) to float on a sea of grog and toddy.

Midnight. *A good New-year! A good New-year! A good New-year!* The wintry cry went from door to door; was repeated a hundred times along the street. The 'first footers' went to their neighbours with lumps of coal and a little gift – that the houses might not lack for fire or food in the year to come.

The small boys chanted the next day:

> *A happy New-year,*
> *A bottle of beer*
> *And a box on the ear*

at the last line giving another boy a blow of the fist, not too hard.

The lighted lamps were set in the windows or tables passing three in the afternoon, in mid-winter.

Red-faced whisky-drinkers sang, or were amorous or sentimental or boastful or angry: so that the small boys were astonished at such queer on-goings.

My father got a glass of whisky at nearly every door he took letters to – but he rationed the offerings out, and so came home merry most evenings till half way through January... He would sing Edwardian music hall songs or evangelical hymns at New Year. He had a good tenor voice.

Swift and marvellous as dreaming, winter passed. It was spring again. The fountains of light leapt higher in the south. Daffodils, larks, lambs were everywhere. The sky grew taller and taller.

The heather hills of Orphir across the bay, were bright-clawed with the muirburn fires at evening.

Suddenly, it was summer. We never questioned why one time of the year was dark, and another bright. Children accept everything, like little princes and princesses; and the fact that nearly all the families were poor had nothing to do with it.

There were long picnicking afternoons at the West-shore, fronting Hoy Sound, with sand in the sandwiches and flies in the tea. In the sun-warmed rockpools little fronds of seaweed floated, and tiny crabs were imprisoned... There a trawler was stuck fast like a fly in treacle in the ebb tide, or, if she chanced to seek Stromness on the flood, she galloped full speed past Graemsay and round Ness.

The girls made long daisy chains. The boys paddled and built formidable castles, moated, till the flood-tide surged in like a terrible army and ruined them.

After the kirk service, in the afternoon, I wandered with my father beyond the kirkyard – that strange peaceful book with stone pages that told the history of Stromness – or along the road on the far side of Brinkie's Brae, a marshy district called the Loons. I lingered impatient while my father spoke to everyone he met; everybody knew him and he knew everybody. He had a quick spark of wit in him that made everyone laugh. 'Oh,' some old woman would say, wiping mirthful eyes, 'Oh, John Broon, it does me heart good to hear thee!'

Every day in the week had its own special flavour. Sunday was all unction

Stromness: 'I open the door to a transfigured world, a white
enchanted Stromness. All the roofs wear tilted white bonnets.'

and piety. But there was a sponge-cake for tea, and a variety of little cakes my
mother had baked at the weekend.

Monday smelt of soap suds and wet wool and linen: being washing day. The
whole day was taken up with that enormous splurge, hot fires and boilers,
clothes flapping in the wind, baskets and wooden pegs. One consolation of
washing day was that always there was ham-and-egg for dinner, and kippers
for tea. (I very much disliked, till a decade later, such diets as mince, stew,
broth, fish. I would have lived entirely on sweeties, toffee, chocolate, given the
choice. A slice of bread spread with Lyle's Golden Syrup, or sprinkled with
sugar, would do.)

Wednesday reeked of the earth, and cows and horses. For then the farmers

Stromness: 'Boys fished with penny lines from the end of the pier.'

came in with beasts to the mart, and stood about the Pier Head, smoking their pipes, making cautious utterances at long intervals.

Saturday, after I went reluctantly to school, tasted of boundless freedom. For that school was a prison, and the teachers were stern or kindly wardresses. The songs we sang in school: even they fell from our lips like little lead birds.

Friday was always a magical day, for it opened the door of the weekend to us.

Tuesday and Thursday had little character. Later, Tuesday brought the *Wizard* to the paper-shop. Thursday afternoon, Stromness went dead, being early closing day. The old folk read the *Orcadian*, after dinner.

Boys fished with penny lines from the end of the pier. Little armies of silver sillocks swarmed along the piers; they were drawn up, flashing and twisting, the hook was eased from their jaws, they gulped themselves to death. Four sillocks for a penny; the boys sold them to old wives who had cats. Some boys caught hundreds and thousands of sillocks in their time. I only caught one, by luck, once.

And sometimes a crab, clown of the sea-bed, was drawn up. And scuttled, panic stricken, back to the pier-verge smelling the lost brine. Or a cruel boy would jump, close-footed, on it; then there was nothing left of the crab but broken bits of shell and a yellow splash on the flagstone.

All the boys ran bare-foot, through the seven holiday weeks.

For a summer or two, we lived in the little 'flatties' or dinghies, rowing here and there across the harbour. We were warned never to row beyond the 'black buoy' at the harbour mouth, lest Hoy Sound sweep our little craft out into the drowning Atlantic.

But we explored the two little green tidal islands – the Holms – that form the east arm of the harbour, with the mysterious ruined house on it.

Ah, there came the *Ola*, riding Hoy Sound superbly on the flood, and turning into the voe. Then the oars must be manned, then we must row out into the *Ola*'s bow waves. Up and down, perilously, went the flattie five or six times, and my heart fluttered in my throat like a bird ... Soon, then, it was time to drift to the home pier for tea.

The one purely ecstatic day of the summer was the release from school for seven or eight weeks. I remember going into a secret place, like the man in the Yeats poem, and exulting. Eight weeks was the next thing to eternity.

But it passed, like a dream of blue and green and gold.

I went with my parents and a brother to Kirkwall in a bus. I had never seen Kirkwall before. It was like going to some place we had read about in a fairy-tale (even though, theoretically, there was great rivalry between the two towns). We met a half-Stromness half-Kirkwall boy and gave him twopence; he came out of a shop with a slice of melon. My father had welcoming words with an ex-Stromness inn-keeper who was now host of the St Ola Hotel in Kirkwall; he gave my brother and me twopence each.

One Sunday each summer my father hired a car and driver and we visited two farms, one in Birsay and one in Evie. The grave courtesy and kindness of the farm-folk showed a kind of life disappearing from the towns even then – the hospitality and the undisguised joy at our visit! Those Orkney farm-folk of two generations ago were natural aristocrats. Generosity and natural courtesy stream through the generations, from very far back. The country people, the animals and cornfields, entered deep into my imagination.

And – back once more in Stromness – we bathed in the sea, from the slipways, or among the Warbeth breakers. One shock of intense coldness, and then happy hours on the hot sand, in and out of the sun-bright rockpools.

Summer went. We began to count on our fingers the few days of freedom left to us. Then – for we went barefoot all summer – we had to sheath our dew-and-seapink feet in stockings and boots, and set out for a higher class-room in the prison of school. We wondered, anxiously, whether the wardress would be kind or strict. New text-books were issued; this session, we would be instructed in the mystery of decimal fractions. Poems like 'The Burial of Sir John Moore at Corunna' and Wordsworth's 'Fidelity' stirred something deep in me. I discovered, to my surprise, that I could write the weekly 'composition' with greater fluency than most of my classmates, though in art and geography and music I was left far behind ... If a boy was made to share a desk with a girl, that was a punishment and an indignity...

> *A boy leaves a small house*
> *Of sea light. He leaves*
> *The sea smells, creel*
> *And limpet and cod.*
>
> *The boy walks between steep*
> *Stone houses, echoing*
> *Gull cries, the all-around*
> *Choirs of the sea,*
>
> *Ship noises, shop noises, clamours*
> *Of bellman and milkcart.*
> *The boy comes at last*
> *To a tower with a tall desk*
>
> *And a globe and a blackboard*
> *And a stern chalk –*
> *-smelling lady. A bell*
> *Nods and summons.*
>
> *A girl comes, cornlight*
> *In the eyes, smelling*

28

*Of peat and cows*
*And the rich midden.*

*Running she comes, late,*
*Reeling in under the last*
*Bronze brimmings. She sits*
*Among twenty whispers.*

Ah, but before the wheel of the year brought in winter again, fell the great Lammas Fair, on the first Tuesday of September. It was kind of Harvest feast – I think Lammas was originally loaf-mass – overbrimming with cornstalks and milk and honey, all the burnished richness of the summer just past. Farmers and their families drove in by bus and gig and horse-and-cart from all the seven parishes in the west, and from Hoy and the south isles: the men in Sunday suits, the girls in flowery dresses. But we town boys weren't concerned with the earth's bounty, only with the things and people that accompanied it: the travelling market-men from the south, with shooting galleries, coconut shies, fortune-telling booth, 'Wall of Death', Indians selling silk out of bulging open cases, cheapjacks, the African prince licking a red-hot poker and lying on a bed of nails, the blind fiddler, the preaching men, the vendors of ice-cream, fruit, lemonade, sweeties, the chirping birds made of wood shavings – and ah! the load of sixpences and pennies in our pockets (for the kind neighbours had given us 'fairings') made us richer than Rockefeller. The dense crowds surged through the streets, and round the Pier Head where the stalls were set up and the market-men cajoled or curled their lips at our bucolic stubbornness. An air of fantasy was abroad – we were all caught up in it. Then at night the roaring naphtha flares were lit among the little magical mushroom village of booths and stalls at the pier-front; and our cup of pure happiness overflowed.

We reeled home, penniless and poor again, and surfeited with sweetness like bees, from the Lammas fields of nectar.

The door of winter was about to open.

# 3
# *Land*

——

*The place before was boggy and thick with stones; but in a short time Earl Magnus's goodness gleamed Godward with such radiance that there came up abundant greenness in the place where he had been killed.*

This miracle of fertility out of barrenness, the desert blossoming as the rose, is a kind of parable of Orkney agriculture. In four thousand years what was originally dark moor – stone and bog everywhere, except where blown shell sand had sweetened the beach-girding soil – has come to wear everywhere the green coat of fertility. Half way up the hills go the plough and the reaper. Sometimes you get the feeling that nowadays too much has been reclaimed; the old wild places, so beautiful in their own way, have been pushed too far back.

> *What would the world be, once bereft*
> *Of wet and wildness? Let them be left,*
> *O let them be left, wildness and wet;*
> *Long live the weeds and the wilderness yet.*
>                                    G. M. Hopkins

Seeking fertile places to settle in: that is what took successive races to Orkney, even (we presume) before the time of agriculture. Sea and lochs and sky teemed with fish and fowl for the hunters; even the shore at ebb-tide was generous.

The first Norsemen to settle peaceably – there had been plenty of red-handed pirates in the preceding centuries from east-over-sea – planned their farms (the 'bu' of the chief) in watered slopes and valleys fronting the sea, like Marwick or Cairston; and there they began the slow arduous business of drainage and digging and quickening.

*Hills for bees to be hived,*
*Beasts kept, a cod-hungry boat,*
*A comfort of fire in the crofts.*
*We furled sails, set firm our feet,*
*Stone laid against stone. . .*
*Dreamed I that darkness*
*Of horse, harp, a hallowed harvest.*

It proved to be a kindly soil, and the country men and women of Orkney have from the beginning been hard workers. It is said that the neolithic inhabitants of Orkney, who existed round the howes of the dead that were so important to them, hardly lived beyond the age of thirty, and their housed bones are twisted with arthritis. In the eighteenth century an Orkneyman was old and bent with labour by the time he was fifty (but perhaps he was healthier than other countrymen who had moved into the new industrial cities; certainly his life had a meaningful pattern, he was bound to the slow fruitful cycle of the year, seed time to harvest). Nowadays Orcadians are materially better off than they have ever been, they are healthy and generally long-lived; but, together with the hard back-breaking toil, much of the old mystery and fulfilment of agricultural life is no longer there. It has vanished with the horse.

*The horse at the shore*
*Casks of red apples, skull, a barrel of rum*

*The horse in the field*
*Plough, ploughman, gulls, a furrow, a cornstalk*

*The horse in the peatbog*
*Twelve baskets of dark fire*

*The horse at the pier*
*Letters, bread, paraffin, one passenger, papers*

*overleaf* Birsay

*The horse at the Show*
*Ribbons, raffia, high bright hooves*

*The horse in the meadow*
*A stallion, a russet gale, between two hills*

*The horse at the burn*
*Quenching a long flame in the throat*

The biggest island of Orkney is called nowadays, insipidly, Mainland; but in Norse times and probably long afterwards on the tongues of country folk it was Hrossey, 'the island of the horse'. The horse was the animal that the farmer used and loved best of all. Without the labour of ox and horse he could hardly have stitched those fertile patches of oats and barley and grass on to the original bleakness. From some of the more barren islands around, where men depended on creel and hook more than the plough, the big island with its many-coloured fields must have seemed, truly, 'the horse island'.

*Our isle is oyster-gray.*
*That patched coat*
*Is the Island of Horses.*

The tractor has long taken over from the horse. There are still old farmers alive who never forgot the strong bond between horse and man; they kept their faithful beasts round the farm until they died of age. We may imagine how some of them felt – and the saddlers and blacksmiths too – when the first tractor stuttered and stank across a field.

*The horsemen are red in the stable*
*With whisky and wrath.*
*The petrol-drinker is in the hills.*

But in general Orcadians took to the machines – cars, tractors, boat-engines, reapers – with as much passion as they will ever allow themselves. The fact that the life blood of the machine – oil – is massively stored under the sea to the east is a source of satisfaction to most modern Orkneymen; though they say

The Orkney landscape today: '...in general Orcadians
took to the machines –'

little about it, one way or the other. Those who have reservations are the environmentalists, the guardians of the heritage; and they tend to be more passionate and articulate.

Slowly the original 'bu' farms grew and begot other farms as more and more of the hill was unlocked by the plough: the 'setters', 'bisters', 'brecks', 'quholms', in all their combinations and varieties. The Norse name-givers were strictly factual – the farm names describe, coldly, the situation of the enclosure, or some outstanding feature or peculiarity of it, or (perhaps for want of any special characteristic) the farm is called by the name of the first farmer... Right up to Orkney's 'agricultural revolution' of only a few generations ago, the cultivated land of a district was enclosed by a turf dyke; beyond the wall ranged the herds of cow and sheep and swine; and so the rigs of bere and oat inside were left all summer to take the sun's burnish. But sometimes, because there were too many people in a 'tunship', the dyke had to be breached so that a patch of dung-fertilised hill land beyond could be put under the plough, and these little enclosures were called 'quoys'. The element 'quoy' is probably the commonest among Orkney farm names.

Coldly descriptive the original farm names were; but now, in the long perspective of time, they have a fascination for all Orkney-lovers. Nowadays, when new houses are built, all kinds of fanciful inappropriate ludicrous names are bestowed on them.

*The old crofts ride a green hill surge,*
*Long arks, men and beasts under one roof.*
*The new bungalows,*
*Will they be there at the dove's return?*

Hugh Marwick's *Orkney Farm Names* is a brilliant exploration of the subject. Another fine book, about the vanished ways of agriculture in Orkney is John Firth's *Reminiscences of an Orkney Parish*.

Hard and anxious the lives of country folk must have been, almost up to the present day. Yet they did not deny themselves festival and fiddle and dance, whenever the time of year for those celebrations came round. The twelve days of Yule (Christmas) were full of elaborate and beautiful ceremonies carried out by the farmer in his own house and outbuildings and fields. The farmer on the morning of the Nativity put a candle in a cow's skull and by the light of this lantern fed his beasts in the byre with more fodder than usual. There is rich beautiful age-old symbolism in what was happening — the fruitful interaction of bread, death, new light... All the ritual element is out of life nowadays, and we are the poorer for it.*

No longer are the midsummer bonfires lit on the summit of every hill in Orkney: a salutation to the sun, an entreaty for the sun's light and kindling to visit this parish and that island, so that, between now and harvest, there would be no blight in the ripening oats. When the fire was at its height, each crofter would light from it his own private torch, and carry it alone through his steading and fields. Till dawn came – and at that time of year sunset and dawn kept the one lamp glowing just under the northern horizon – there was eating and drinking and dancing, and the young men leapt like heroes through the flames.

We have had to give up a great deal of the richly ceremonial in order to arrive at our present state of security and affluence. Who nowadays would give up his car, his colour TV, his holiday in the sun, to dance round a fire on midsummer's eve, or greet the animals on a Yule morning with the 'light-out-of-death' lantern? Orkney's agricultural revolution began nearly two centuries ago, and it has completely altered the appearance of the islands, and their prosperity; and perhaps the very nature of the people.

It began when the lairds suddenly found themselves poor, with the collapse of the kelp trade. No longer did the smoke of burning seaweed rise in summer from the stone pits along the shore. What, at all events, had countrymen to do with such artificial trade, subject to all the fluctuations of world commerce?

The landlords *had* to make their acres pay, or else live in crumbling poverty-stricken mansions.

Like the tide coming in, here fast, there reluctantly, the land improvements took place. (One of the greatest obstacles to improvement was the conservative attitude of the crofters themselves; to those who have won so precarious a foothold in time, any change must seem likely to be for the worse.) Enclosures, rotation of crops, division of the common land, introduction of new breeds of cattle, sheep, horses, the bringing in by the lairds of progressive farmers from

*The ceremonies recorded are from Shetland, but the two island groups were so close, in geography and race and culture, that Orkney must have shared them.

37

the south to manage the large home farms – these gradually accomplished a change for the better. At the end of the nineteenth century there was 250 per cent more arable land in Orkney than at the beginning.

Even so, the situation of the crofters and small tenants continued to be precarious. They were at the mercy of the lairds, both as regards their rent and their period of tenure (they could be put out of their holdings at very short notice; they had no inducement to improve their steadings or widen the patch of green round about).

An act of parliament of 1886 altered everything in their favour. Fair rents were imposed – arrears of rent reduced or wiped out. They were secure from sudden arbitrary eviction. If for some reason they did leave their holdings, the landlord had to compensate them adequately for any improvements they had carried out.

The position of the lairds was very much weakened by the same act. Slowly, the large estates (or most of them) were split up and sold to the small farmers and crofters who now occupied their own independent holdings. Henceforth they were completely independent of all but weather, pest, and the laws of supply and demand.

Still, here and there on the islands, are the 'big houses' of the lairds. They have fine situations; some of the older houses are very beautiful; some of the Victorian ones more vulgar and brash.

The Crofters Holdings (Scotland) Act of 1886 was the basis of Orkney's present agricultural prosperity.

Slowly the green encroached on heath and moor. Larger sturdier sheep and cattle moved on the new fertile hillsides.

In the first sixty years of this century the number of cattle has doubled, and the number of sheep has more than doubled. (And we should not forget that the sheep and the cattle were quite other, in size and yield, than the miserable 'bestial' described by Rev George Barry in 'Nature Anthology' in the present book.) It was otherwise, alas, with the poor horse. It came, because of the machines, within an ace of 'a final solution'. Is it illusion, or are there more horses in our summer fields than there were two decades ago? Like the horses in Edwin Muir's great poem of that name, perhaps these faithful animals – in spite of the ill that has been done them – refuse to break the ancient treaty with men.

Detail, Melsetter House, Hoy: '. . . some of the older houses are very beautiful;'

It has been found, too, that grass crops are more suited to our soil and climate than the traditional oats, bere, barley. While the new green of grass takes over, increasingly, from the bog and hill – and this crop, at the times of ripeness and cutting, makes marvellous vivid strips of colour – the number of farms and farmers decreases. The tendency is for smaller farms to be gradually absorbed into bigger units; and the government actively encourages this thinning out with what's called a 'copper handshake' to the small farmer who surrenders his few acres. Increasing mechanisation has made this development unavoidable.

Other improvements have been the spread of electricity all over the country-side, so that now only the most remote places are without it (but not for much longer), and various water schemes that have done away with the laborious getting of water from well or burn, several times a day. (It can be argued, of course, that the more easily available the necessities of life are, the less we appreciate them: water on tap is at last only a tasteless liquidity.) But most Orkney country-folk still appreciate their fire: with their thews and sweat they dig the peat from the bog as their remote ancestors did. Perhaps if coal and electricity were not so expensive, the peat-bogs would be empty of workers in early summer too. Meantime we still have, all over the Orkney countryside at all seasons, the enchanting aroma of peat-smoke at the open doors.

In two centuries Orkney agriculture has come a long way. Yet strong links with the past endure; in some farms the same families have tilled the earth continuously for nine hundred years; and in others for periods almost as long.

To see the Orkney country folk in relaxed mood, go to the Agricultural show in Dounby, where the three parishes meet, in early August. The sense of imminent harvest is in the air. All around the village of Dounby, the fields are green, or heavy with burnish. On display, in a single square field, are all the finest produce of the Orkney farms; powerful ponderous bulls, silky rich-uddered cows, sheep marvellously fleeced, cocks that give the sun a rousing salute every few minutes. In the marquees are dispensed the produce of the farm kitchens – bannocks, scones, rhubarb jam, pancakes, buns of every kind. If you would enjoy the Orkney farmers in the flavour of a unique humour and in their miracles of understatement, the whisky tent is the place to go: you are experiencing immemorial country flavours, listening to the authentic tongue-music of a thousand years and more. 'A fair field full of folk' – the Dounby Show is a democratic assembly; every kind and condition of Orkney men and

Clydesdale getting ready for the Agricultural Show in Dounby.

women are there, in addition to the farmers and the farm folk – laird, clerks, mechanics, shop-keepers, tourists, 'the professional classes', babies, white-beards, fair-ground men, drunks – a tumultuous throng, a gay surging patch-work. For that one bright day in the busy year, it seems that all the people of Orkney have come together to wonder and to celebrate.

# 4
# *Kirkwall*

═══

The 'Kirk' part of Kirkwall is not St Magnus Cathedral, but an earlier church dedicated to St Olaf, a few stones of which still stand in a close off Bridge Street. 'Wall' is in fact a corruption of 'voe' (bay). Pedants and map-makers wreaked havoc in our place names at that very sensitive period when place names were becoming fixed. One went so far as to call the main island 'Pomona', which no Orcadian before or since has used; except that one delectable hostelry in Finstown bears the name.

Kirkwall was first mentioned in *Orkneyinga Saga* when the first Earl Rognvald (Brusison) had a house or a hall there. Rognvald must have been a lucky name to bear; this Rognvald Brusison was as attractive and accomplished in his way as the second Earl Rognvald (Kolson). But both died suddenly and violently.

This first Rognvald had the ill-luck to fall out with the man who ruled Orkney jointly with him: his uncle Earl Thorfinn, who was probably the most talented governor ever to rule the islands – Thorfinn's sovereignty extended deep into Scotland, and as far as the Hebrides and Man. Aided by his friend the King of Norway, Earl Rognvald came suddenly on Thorfinn at his hall in Orphir and put torches to it. Among the ashes and charred bones next morning it was presumed that Thorfinn lay. In fact he had taken his wife Ingibiorg in his arms and broken through the smoke and flames, and rowed to Caithness in a small boat.

Assuming that now he was sole lord of Orkney, the young earl with some of his men set out in a boat for the little island of Papa Stronsay. It was the midwinter of 1046. They intended to buy malt for the Yule brewing. Behind him in Kirkwall he left the warriors loaned him by the King in the east: an

St Magnus Cathedral, Kirkwall.

elite corps. The house in Papa Stronsay was surrounded in the night and set on fire. The earl, garbed like a priest, leapt over the heads of the besiegers, but his little dog, trying to protect him at the shore, barked frantically and drew Thorfinn's burners. They put their daggers into him and made an end: the rocks were red with seaweed and blood.

Thorfinn and his men returned to Kirkwall in Rognvald's boat. Down to the shore came the Norwegian bodyguard to greet their friend, unarmed. There and then they were set upon and slaughtered – all but one man who was given leave to take that piece of new-minted history back to the King in Bergen.

Thus, violently, the story of Kirkwall begins. In the centuries that followed, the growing town was to see other acts of violence: the siege of the castle, murder in the high street, the hanging and burning of sheep-thief and witch. Nowadays all that 'wild wark' (as they say in Orkney) is contained in an unique football game played each Christmas Day and New Year's Day between the 'uppies' and the 'doonies'. It is an anarchical game, with no rules or set number of players: back and fore the mostly invisible 'ba' is hustled by the closely-meshed teams, until sooner or later it is flung into the sea (a 'doonie' victory) or brought to a wall in the Laverock (an 'uppie' gain). Once, fancifully, I wrote a piece about the origin of the game: how a Yule-tide squabble in the fifteenth century between earl's men (down-the-gates) and bishop's men (up-the-gates) led to a young dandy having his head cut off: whereupon both sides tried desperately to get hold of it, one lot to bring it to the bishop as proof of murder, the other mob to hustle and bury the incriminating thing deep in the sea . . . But probably the Ba' game is much older: it may be a dramatised myth – the forces of winter and summer, heather and tilth, ice and fire, struggling to possess the sun.

It is easy to see why the first Rognvald chose Kirkwall to build his hall. One glance at the map shows how almost exactly Kirkwall lies at the heart of Orkney – at the point of intersection between North Isles and South Isles, East Mainland and West Mainland. It had the advantage too of having a fine lagoon (now called the Peerie Sea, and much shrunken from its former bounds) where ships could shelter at any season. Men coming and going about their business, by sea or land, were likely to pass in or near Kirkwall: a market town, sooner or later, was bound to take root there. For an earl it must have been the ideal administrative centre.

And yet the great Earl Thorfinn who had Rognvald done to death in the Papa Stronsay ebb chose to rule from Birsay in the north-west of Mainland (some say his palace was on the little steep green tidal island called Brough of Birsay). There too the Bishop had his little cathedral kirk. Perhaps the great earl associated Kirkwall too much with Rognvald, and so turned his back on it. Birsay, of course, is a beautiful place, perhaps the most pleasant and fruitful region in all Orkney. The next three generations of earls – Paul and Erlend, Hakon and Magnus, Harald and Paul – continued, we presume, to rule from Birsay or Orphir or elsewhere. Meantime the little market village continued to grow. There men exchanged news and bits of silver, dried fish and sacks of corn, Irish linen and Norse timber. There the little kirk of Saint Olaf gave sweet tongue with its bell on a feast day.

It was the eye of the second Earl Rognvald, St Magnus's nephew, that picked on 'kirk-bay' village to be his capital. It was he who ordered the building of the great cathedral of St Magnus that still stands almost unscathed – a miracle when one thinks of the tempests of history it has weathered. The first blocks of red sandstone from quarries near and far were being set in place when Rognvald Kolson departed with fifteen ships on his great crusade of 1151–54. When he got back from Jerusalem, Constantinople, Rome, the great stone rose would be breaking from its bud. There, in a huge pillar, the bones of St Magnus were brought from Birsay and ceremonially immured.

The history of Kirkwall – rich and tumultuous for so small a city – has been marvellously and meticulously recorded in a fine book published locally at the end of last century – Hossack's *Kirkwall in the Orkneys*.

The Cathedral endures, but many buildings as striking in their way have withered or vanished down the centuries. The Castle is no more. The Bishop's Palace where Hakon died, a broken king after Largs, is a towered ruin. A ruin beautiful in spite of its dilapidation is the Earl's Palace nearby, exquisitely built by the architects of the seventeenth-century Stuart Earl of Orkney, Patrick: a Machiavellian creature, it seems, who had nevertheless a fine taste in the arts.

It was about Patrick Stuart's time and afterwards, that Orkney had its great crop of witches – women old and young who, because of some physical malformation or quirk of character, drew parish gossip about themselves; or perhaps some of them did indulge in the ancient pre-Christian fertility rites that they thought necessary to keep the precarious wheel of agriculture fruitfully

'The Bishop's Palace, where Hakon died, a broken king after Largs,
is a towered ruin.'

turning. Many of them met a wretched end – they had 'the red sark putten on
them' – at the place called Gallowsha' (at the top of the steep road now called
Clay Loan).

Gallowsha'

*Three Old Women*
'Bring in fire!' three old women cried. 'Give her the yellow and red coat!'
But no torches were lit before the throat was girdled.

*Neighbour*
Was as bonny a bairn as ever wore daisies, she. What worm comes in at the
mouth when innocence sleeps? It breeds in the heart.

*The Stranger*
Oh yes, but she cried. She skirled when she saw the post and the rope! She
stopped then. She went to the hangman laughing like to a bridegroom.

*Preacher*
Repent ye, therefore, and turn. Behold the tree of sinners, that the rose petals
thereof melt as snow, and are thorns and ashes soon.

*Ale-wife*
Ale, penny a pot. Cool the flame the poor girl stands in. Usque, twopence the
glass. Warm a cold spirit. It passes.

*A Palace Guard*
He tried her this way and that, with smiles and sovereigns, then threatenings.
She would not abide his cajolings under the moon. Then three strangers, with
paper and seal, stood at her father's door.

*Child*
What's that black mask? What white thing is shaking under the rope? Mother,
why seven torches, and the sun so bright?

Famous men – kings, writers, statesmen, warriors – have visited Kirkwall and
gone again. One wonders what went through the mind of King James the Fifth
as he stepped ashore from the little boat: only a few years before these islanders,
confused in their loyalties, bereft of the protection of their ancient laws, resentful
of the Scots who were lording it over them increasingly, had taken up arms

and resoundingly beaten the royal army at Summerdale. King James brought unguents and salves: he revived the people's pride by giving Kirkwall royal burgh status (it was already a city by virtue of its cathedral).

Sir Walter Scott lingered in Kirkwall in 1814; for some reason he took a distaste to the town, and wrote an insulting little poem about it.

Tennyson and Gladstone arrived on a ship, Russia-bound. They were at once offered the Freedom of the City. Tennyson, wrapped in gloom, declined to speak at the ceremony, but the Prime Minister with his great rolling periods more than made up for that lack. The Poet Laureate left no lines about the city or the islands (one thinks that his interest might have been kindled a little by Orkney's place in the Arthurian cycle).

In a real sense Kirkwall has no need of imported fame: she has nurtured a wealth of scholars and artists. The poets Edwin Muir and Robert Rendall and Duncan J. Robertson went to school here, and Stanley Cursiter the Queen's Limner. About the turn of the century, Kirkwall Grammar School produced an astonishing crop of talent. Local boys and boys from the parishes and islands around passed on to one or other of the Scottish Universities, and after distinguished achievements there became professors in Britain and in almost every part of the empire. It is noteworthy perhaps that most of these brilliant men chose scientific disciplines: medicine, agriculture, botany, geology. Some people, like Dr Hugh Marwick, have argued that the Orcadian mind is practical rather than imaginative. The wealth of island culture from the beginning contradicts this; we should rather see the Orkney mind as an intermeshing of the practical and the imaginative, and this has been a constant pattern. The broch builders united supreme utility with a fine sense of form and structure. The Norsemen sailed to get Irish linen and girls, French wine-barrels, English silver, in ships of superb design . . . Indeed, what is a poem or a carving on a stone? It was, originally, a spell to make the corn grow, to lure fish into the net; beauty and utility were one.

Nowadays, Kirkwall is a busy town. It seems all of Orkney is to be found there, on a Monday or a Saturday afternoon. Kirkwall continues to grow, while the parishes and islands are drained slowly of their populations. In the kind of centralising society that is the universal pattern nowadays, this imbalance is perhaps inevitable. But still many Orcadians wonder if it makes for the health of the total community.

A significant development of recent years has been the settling in Orkney of scores of families from the south, mainly England; they have come to rediscover old wholesome cycles of life that industrialism has been destroying for two centuries, and now with ever-increasing ruthlessness. But with oil flowing into Flotta from the North Sea, and an as-yet-untapped uranium belt in the Stromness-Sandwick area, no one can say how Orkney will look in the next half-century or so. Meantime, the great majority of the immigrants have settled down well with the Orcadians: within a generation, they should add a new rich strain to the already complex blood-strain of Orkney.

Visitors to Orkney must be surprised at the number of banks and building societies in Kirkwall especially. This is the modern equivalent of the ancient 'stocking under the bed'. The Orcadians have always been a prudent penny-wise people; which however has nothing to do with lack of generosity. On the farms especially, they cannot load enough food or drink on the table for guests or strangers.

On the outskirts of Kirkwall are two distilleries: Highland Park and Scapa. They both produce a uniquely flavoured malt whisky, that is becoming increasingly popular all over the world.

Supermarkets, banks, shops, hotels, busy piers and streets, the large web of government offices, housing schemes, hostels: Kirkwall is the busy heart of Orkney indeed. Inside the town there are places where you can escape the market-day bustle and rush: Tankerness House with its marvellous little museum and, behind, a wide garden, rich in summer with blossom and bees, where you can sit and linger. Across the street, in the roseate gloom of St Magnus Cathedral, you step into history. How did the interior of St Magnus look four and a half centuries ago, when one of our greatest bishops, Robert Reid (he founded Edinburgh University) reorganised the chapter? Some think that then, at the height of its glory, the cathedral was richly painted and ornamented, quite unlike the dim martyr-glow we move reverently through nowadays. Would there have been vivid Stations of the Cross along walls now studded with mournful seventeenth- and eighteenth-century tombstones? Between then and now, the Cathedral has suffered indignities – whitewash, Cromwell's horses, a storing of merchants' masts and spars... Some people think St Magnus would be better now without the tombstones, and especially without the massive Victorian memorials to Baikie and Rae, explorers. For all

Scapa distillery workers, Richard Burton, Richard Burton Jr and
Willie Fraser, stowing newly filled casks in the warehouse, which
in three years time will produce a uniquely flavoured malt whisky.

its immense hewn power, St Magnus should be seen too as a work of marvellous delicacy that can be spoiled by thoughtless tamperings.

Not so very long ago, on late summer evenings, the booths of the Lammas Market did their raucous flare-lit business in the shadow of the cathedral; until magistrates, fearful of irreverence, moved the coconut-men and cheap-jacks and fortune-tellers to a field in the outskirts. But all life – business, religion, fantasy – is a single weave, and we sunder it at our peril, perhaps. Of recent years, a St Magnus Fair has been initiated, and has already sent down roots; it too plies its tumultuous business just under the red walls of 'the old kirk', and all profits go to the maintenance of the cathedral itself – in recent years strains and cracks have been found in the fabric.

The midsummer St Magnus Festival of the arts, begun in 1977, is now firmly established in the Orkney calendar. Much of the music is performed inside the Cathedral. The main item of the opening festival was Peter Maxwell Davies' chamber opera *The Martyrdom of St Magnus*.

People come from all over Britain, and beyond, to attend the festival. The leading British journals and magazines give it generous space. Orkney, after long centuries, is once more a living centre of the arts.

# 5
## Sea

---

*Salt in the mouth,*
*The rage*
*Of north wind at morning,*
*Sodden crust,*
*Cold kissings of rain.*
*This unease*
*Is better than Ragna at her hearth.*

*Too late for rudder's turning*
*Back into history,*
*The old worn web,*
*King, lawman, merchant, serf.*
*The prow crashes*
*Into a new time.*

*They will say next winter*
*At the fire,*
*'Leif Ericson went*
*The fool's voyage.'*
*A man will sing to a harp,*
*'Heroes*
*Do not venture only for bits of gold.'*
*An old woman will say*
*To girls at candle-time,*
*'It is that slut, the sea*

'The Swan's Path', 'the whale road': with such kennings the Norsemen set out on the circling magnificence of the sea. What made them sail west from Norway was a complex thing: political and economic pressures, an insatiable curiosity, a lust for domination. They were marvellous seamen, venturing without compass in frail beautiful boats. They came to the snow and fires of Iceland. They even, for a time (until the climate worsened), wrung a livelihood from the bleakness of Greenland. Westwards still they went, and came on the painted feathered Indians and the wild grapes of North America, four centuries before Columbus.

Their longships had, long before, probed among the Shetlands and the Orkneys. The islands were inhabited by a dark sturdy imaginative people. The Vikings opened the place up with axe and fire, took what they wanted, and sailed off again. This must have happened time after time – a monotonous blood-splashed pattern. Yet they never forgot the fertility of the islands: fish, birds, corn. At last they came as settlers and farmers. What happened to the native Picts can only be imagined; at best they were enslaved and their women taken; the conquerors' story in the next few centuries is brilliantly told in *Orkneyinga Saga*.

In a cluster of islands like Orkney sea and land – stark opposites, irrec-oncilable – are inextricably mingled. They take richness and beauty from one another: the fish and the cornstalk, peatfire and fish-oil lamp, in one croft. The first Orcadians, whoever they were, tried to explain the mysterious unity of sea and land with a web of legend. The seals with their large eloquent eyes and love of music are the link. They come ashore, cast their skins, dance on the sand in human form. A man, concealed in the long grass above, steals a pelt, and so the selkie lass cannot go back to her element; she is his, a croft-wife, till she dies or finds after many years her skin hidden in the barn rafters . . . or else a country girl sweet as milk is taken to Suleskerry or Hether Blether the vanishing island by the seal-tribe, and never seen again.

The golden age of Orkney lasted three centuries or thereby: the great explorers, vikings, pilgrims were at last pearl and coral or kirkyard dust. The next few centuries certainly had its sailors, fishermen, beachcombers, but they

Grey seal: 'They come ashore, cast their skins, dance on the sand
in human form.'

have no names or stories. What emerges starkly is the people's ambivalent attitude to the sea. The sea was the great mother: she gave them, sometimes lavishly, sometimes stingily, from her stores of fish, whale, salt, tangle, drift-wood. Winter after winter she hurled freighted ships on the rocks and crags; while the cargoes of rum or wheat or apples lasted, life in this island and that was a long winter festival. But the sea did not give for nothing; another of her names was 'the widow-maker'. From time to time the sea took a single life to herself, or at a stroke a whole ship's crew. And this was her due. Therefore, a man struggling in the sea need look for small help from those on shore; if he got to land, good and well; if he drowned, the sea was taking what was hers. In fact, it was dangerous and foolish to try to save a sea-embroiled man: the would-be rescuer was sure to suffer grievously for his presumption.

This primitive double attitude to the sea, provider and destroyer, faded well over a century ago. The achievement of the Orkney lifeboats in the last hundred years is unequalled for resource and heroism. Tragedy in 1969 struck the Longhope lifeboat going to rescue a ship in difficulties: the entire crew was lost; within a few days a new crew of life-savers had volunteered.

The coast of Orkney is no longer a graveyard for ships. A scattering of lighthouses keeps benighted or storm-shaken ships on their safe sure ways.

There are hundreds of fascinating sea stories told in the islands: of smugglers, Armada survivors, King Hakon and Largs, the press-gang that terrorised Orkney crofts during the Napoleonic wars, the pirate Gow, the witches who sold good winds to skippers, merchants, fishermen, beachcombers, storm-watching women, whalers, Hudson's Bay traders, emigrants, Cook and Franklin who drew barrels of water at Logins Well in Stromness, the sinking of *Hampshire* and *Royal Oak*, the suicide in midsummer 1919 of the entire German Grand Fleet in Scapa Flow. A very moving story is of the death of a little Queen on shipboard on the North Sea.

*The ship rode at anchor in the calm of a little voe.*

*The ship had limped out of the North Sea the day before, late: salt-encrusted, sail-torn.*

*Some of the islanders had come down to the shore, mostly women. The men were more cautious: they could see the foreign heraldry of Scotland on the stern. Strange ships meant, usually, trouble. The men waited round the crofts, ready to take to the hills.*

*But one man stood at the shore, slightly apart from the women. He was the farmer from The Bu, the chief man in the island.*

*From the shore they could see men on the ship, going about their business, but slowly, as if they were sailors in a gray sea dream. The sailors paid small attention to the island and the people on the shore.*

*A man in a gray cloak had stood since dawn at the helm: slowly he gestured here and there; slowly the sailors obeyed him. Needles were put into the torn sail. The salt scabs were scrubbed and washed from the handsome oak of the vessel.*

*Once the skipper at the helm turned his face shorewards. He raised his hand. The farmer, the laird, raised his hand in reply.*

*The women formed a circle then. They broke the long silence. Their faces were here and there. Their voices were sharp with inquisition.*

*The sun rose higher.*

*There was a dead child cradled in the ship, in a little oak-panelled cabin. Her hair was tangled like storm-beaten corn.*

*The dead girl lay on a narrow bed in the middle of the ship-chamber. She was clad in white linen. The sun came in at the cabin window and shone foursquare across her.*

*The cabin smelt still of spindrift and flung weed, but country airs too came in at the window now. All was in order, except that one of the lamps had been half-wrenched from its wall-bracket. It hung, twisted, just above the door.*

*The women in this death-room began to move. They moved even slower than the sailors outside on rigging and forecastle. It was as if they bent and turned to unheard harps.*

*One gathered the wild hair of the child and made a bright knot of it and tied it in a white ribbon. The other two took from a carved chest under the bed a long gown: it was blue satin, it was sewn about the bodice with hundreds of little pearls, it had silver clasps at shoulder and waist. After they had raised the small stiff body they sheathed it in the magnificent fabric. Then, once more, they crossed the thin hands one upon the other.*

*The dead child was as remote as a star: a first star in the new darkness of autumn, at harvest-time, that glitters magnificent and cold in a pool.*

*One of the women took a crystal phial from the sea-chest. She shook drops on to her long fingers. She touched, here and there, the face and broidered hair of the dead child.*

*The second woman smiled.*

*Late in the afternoon the skipper of the ship had himself rowed ashore in a small blue boat.*

*He walked up the beach to the farmer who stood, still, on the sea-bank above. The women hovered around, like gulls about a half-broken crust.*

*The skipper said to the laird: 'You are wondering no doubt what brings a strange ship into your bay. Sir, I ought to have informed you sooner. Other concerns prevented courtesy. We have come from Bergen in Norway. We are bound for Leith in Scotland. Between Norway and Scotland we ran into a storm, one of the worst I have experienced, and I am an old sailor. We carried the Queen of Scotland across the North Sea to her people and her throne. It was foreseen that some day she would be Margaret, Queen of Scotland and of England and of Norway also. Sir, she was a tender child of seven years, and the storm that made me gray in the face was the end of her.'*

*The laird shook his head in wonderment.*

*The women covered their heads. The wailing was spun from mouth to mouth: a thin gray web of grief.*

That harbour, seven hundred years later, is called, still, St Margaret's Hope.

Now the islands are connected to each other, and to Scotland, by comfortable and efficient ferry-boats. The fishermen no longer sail alone to the creels in little yawls, for meagre uncertain returns. The modern fishing boats are bigger, well-manned, and relatively prosperous.

Occasionally, on the horizon, the islands see the long silhouette of a tanker bound for Flotta and the oil tanks.

Units of the NATO fleet come and go in Scapa Flow, until recently the most famous anchorage in the hemisphere.

Only children nowadays take seriously and wonderingly the old legends of the seal-girl stolen to work in peatbank and furrow, of the croft girl sea-enchanted to selkie ways. There is one beautiful true story that sums up perhaps the hardships and charities of man in his dealings with the sea; it is one of the most moving episodes in *Orkneyinga Saga*. A Shetland crofter waits at the shore for his mate to come out fishing, in vain. It was dangerous to fish alone, in the fierce off-shore tide. A man in a white hood – a stranger – hails him. He offers to row while the crofter-fisherman works the lines. The offer is accepted, but soon the poor fisherman wishes he had never seen the hooded man; for he rows at once into the fiercest whirls and tugs of the tide-stream, where the boat dances like a cork. (But there the best, strongest fish are to be found.) A basketful is perilously taken, then the oarsman rows with skill and power for the shore, where a group of women are waiting. The catch is divided. The cowled stranger gives his fish to the waiting women; then, as he turns away, he

'The harbour, seven hundred years later, is called, still,
St Margaret's Hope.'

stumbles on a slippery stone, and the women laugh. The man picks himself up, replies with an impromptu poem on the harp of his mouth, the last line of which is, 'Who'd know that I was an earl? . . . ' It is common knowledge before nightfall that the mysterious man is the great Earl Rognvald Kolson. The story encapsulates the astonishing character of the man in all its facets: his humour, his daring, his charity, his gift for spontaneous poetry. It also illustrates what the sea means perennially to those who live beside it: danger, sudden bounty, trust, uncertainty, hunger. The crofter-fisherman, we presume, stayed at home with his plough and his few creels. Earl Rognvald was about to launch into the greatest venture of his lie: the sea-pilgrimage to Jerusalem, Byzantium, Rome, in which piety and ancient Viking barbarism were so curiously mixed.

# 6
## *Stromness*

There must always have been people living in or near Stromness. The inner end of the harbour was called Hamnavoe, 'the haven inside the bay'; so early fishermen knew it was a good place to keep their boats. The district to the north-east is called Cairston, a fertile stretch with fine farms on it, and, below, clusters of seals on the rocks. Indeed, the Castle of Cairston comes into *Orkneyinga Saga*; the people inside were besieged one Michaelmas; one man ran from the imminent storm of fire and axes all the way to Kirkwall, and didn't stop until his shield wedged in the wide door of the Cathedral.

The first recorded house was an inn at the very tip of the long blue tongue of sea that is the harbour, in 1580. The hosts were William and Mareon Clark. They had 'power of brewing and selling, keiping of ostelrie and bying of all thingis apperteining thairto for furnissing of the commounes and utheris resorting thairaway...'

It is not likely that William Clark would open an inn for fishermen and farm folk, who lived on their own produce and refreshment. Large ships, many of them foreign, were beginning to drop anchor behind the two little sheep islands, the Holms, that form the eastern arm of the harbour. That entry in a lawyer's ledger is all we know about William and Mareon, the first recorded townsfolk. But the imagination delights to work on them.

> *Your door stood open wide*
> *From the rising of the lark*
> *To the pole of night, to all men,*
> *William and Mareon Clark.*

59

*You gathered about your fires*
*The crew of the wintered barque*
*From Lisbon, or Brest, or Boston,*
      *William and Mareon Clark.*

*Tired, you'd put out the lamps*
*Cover the fire, and hark!*
*A scatter of hooves on the cobbles.*
      *William and Mareon Clark . . .*

*Nothing. You cannot hear us.*
*Two names, quilled and stark*
*On a lawyer's parchment, ghostings –*
      *William and Mareon Clark . . .*

Once a nucleus had formed, the little village (called variously then Hamnavoe, Cairston, Stromness) grew rapidly. It was not an easy place to build houses on. The granite hill called Brinkie's Brae slopes steeply from the west into the harbour. Out of the flank of Brinkie's Brae the new house foundations had to be hewn. On small stone piers protruding into the sea other houses were reared, gable-ended to the cold east and the winter sea-spray. One gets the impression that on a man's little enclosure or 'quoy' he crammed in as many houses as he could, to grow rich on the rents. Yet the pattern of the town is beautiful, without (it seems) there being any overall plan in the minds of the merchants and landowners who threw it together so hurriedly and inconsiderately.

*The street uncoiled like a sailor's rope from North to*
    *South*
*And closes swarmed up the side of the hill*
*Among gardens and clouds,*
*And closes stepped down to the shifting water*
*And the nets and whitemaas . . .*

The eighteenth century was Stromness's golden age. The recurring wars with France meant that much shipping sailed round the north of Britain, since the

Stromness: 'One gets the impression that on a man's little enclosure
or "quoy" he crammed in as many houses as he could, to grow
rich on the rents.'

English Channel was unsafe. The shop-keepers grew wealthy on kroner, marks, doubloons, escudos: by this time Stromness was known all over Europe to be a safe anchorage from storms and privateers.

One young man about this time disgraced the name of Stromness. A local merchant, William Gow, had a son called John, who (like hundreds of his Orkney contemporaries) went to sea when he was still a lad. That was the last that was heard of him, until in the winter of 1725 an armed merchant-ship called the *George* anchored in Cairston Roads. The skipper stepped ashore, and he turned out to be John Gow. At once he was welcomed into the best local houses; he and the daughter of a local merchant fell in love, and exchanged pledges. The ordinary townsfolk, however, were disconcerted by the behaviour of Gow's crew, a patchwork of ruffians recruited (it seemed) from the sleaziest waterfronts of Britain. They fought, thieved, threatened, made rout and riot everywhere, molested the young women. By chance Gow's ship was recognised by a storm-bound skipper: she was really the *Revenge*, a pirate vessel that had been terrorising the North Atlantic all the preceding year. Gow, desperately attempting to escape the trap that was closing in, drove his ship against the Calf of Eday in the northern Orkneys; he was captured, tried and executed in London with the worst of his shipmates in the summer of 1726. A dreadful story came to light as the trial unfolded: a mutiny in the Mediterranean on the ship *Caroline*, bound from Santa Cruz to Genoa: Captain Ferneau and all his officers murdered, except Ferneau's loved and trusted officer John Gow, to whom he had entrusted the key of the arms-chest.

As if to compensate for Gow, only a few years later history gave Stromness its hero, a merchant called Alexander Graham. In those days the merchants of all small ports in Scotland had to pay cess-money to the royal burghs before they could engage in trade. So Stromness was in thrall, to this extent, to Kirkwall. Graham, with great skill and determination, organised his fellow-merchants to refuse payment of the cess. Court action after court action ended, many years later, in the House of Lords: a victory for Stromness and Graham, but not only for them, for all the many Scottish ports similarly bled by the royal burghs. A few years later Graham died in poverty; he had ruined himself with legal costs. There is not even a gravestone to him in the kirkyard.

There was an old hag of nearly a hundred who lived in a hovel on the side of Brinkie's Brae when a lawyer and poet and lighthouse commissioner called

Walter Scott came to Orkney on the lighthouse ship *Pharos* in 1814. His poetry, though popular and romantic, did not pay. Now he was on the lookout for plots for novels. He was told that Bessie Millie, the old storm-brewer, remembered John Gow well. She told him enough to set his imagination working: a few years later the fruits of the seed sown that day in Stromness appeared, a novel called *The Pirate*, in which the poor old Stromness witch who sold favourable winds to sailors at sixpence a time became the towering sibyl Norna of Fitful Head.

Pirate and hero and witch flourished in the eighteenth century. The next century is empty of names, but Stromness continued to grow and prosper. Ships of the Hudson's Bay Company called at Stromness for a last provisioning, and also to take to the trading posts of Canada young Orkneymen who had otherwise little outlet for their energies in the overcrowded crofts of home. They turned out to be good workers. Many of them made substantial fortunes in 'the nor-west'. Many never saw Orkney again; but such surnames as Flett, Foubister, Folster, linger still among the Canadian Indians . . . Whalers too called at Stromness to complete their crews; their wages, when they got home from the Davis Straits about harvest time, were welcome in the hand-to-mouth crofts . . . There were one or two boom years in Stromness, also, when vast herring harvests were landed. But the sea, as always, gave her treasures capriciously. Lean and hungry seasons followed the years of the endless silver torrents, and at last this uncertain traffic came to an end.

Across the bay from Stromness is the Hall of Clestrain. In that big house was born the Orkney explorer Dr John Rae. When, in the mid-nineteenth century, the two ships *Erebus* and *Terror* seeking for the elusive 'north-west passage' vanished, the whole nation quickened with interest and speculation. (It was the great age of mapping the blank areas of the globe.) What had happened to the famous navigator Sir John Franklin? It was Rae and his Orkneymen who discovered the truth, from the mouth of an Eskimo. The thick short fish-smelling smiling one produced, as evidence, forks and coins and sashes taken from the ice-doomed sailors. The two great ships had been crushed like matchwood in the bergs and floes. (Incidentally, Stromness had been the last port and watering-place of the Franklin expedition.)

*overleaf* Stromness

63

*In the ice village, no information.*
*We must first sit at a fish-board*
*Lit with smiles . . .*
*'In the House of Ice (he said)*
*Iron and oak are frail flowers, bone*
*Is subtle and lasting.*
*Our creatures came kindly about the strangers.*
*Birds, fish offered help.*
*They could not understand. The greeting*
*Withered in the air.*
*They could not reply, laughing,*
Come, caribou. Come, wolf. Come, snow-bird.
*They were ghosts before death*
*One after another, drifting*
*In bright and dark circles, untrysted.*
*We watched, just under the horizon' . . .*

James Watt, when he watched his mother's kettle boiling, foreshadowed (among many marvels of the Industrial Age) the decline of Stromness. The ugly steam ships when they came had not such need as the old beautiful sailing ships of shelter and provisioning. Gradually the pulse of the town slowed down. The population dwindled. The boat-building yards and the coopers' yards fell silent. Herring stations were abandoned. The distillery that produced the famous 'Old Orkney' malt whisky closed its doors. The period between the two world wars was the bleakest time in Stromness's history. Young people who grew up then had a sense of decline and stagnation. Even the public houses, fifty years before so numerous along the street, had had to put up their shutters.

The outlook is much brighter now. There is boat-building again, bigger fishing craft in the west and a better market for the fish, toffee-making, a thriving tourist industry; a sense of stir and purpose everywhere.

What can never be taken away from the town is a unique beauty. The stone web will always be there between Brinkie's Brae and the sea. The single surging twisting street is admired by all visitors to Stromness. But what they too seldom visit are the closes that swarm up the side of the hill, and the steps that seek down to the twenty creeled and salty piers, washed twice a day by cold incoming Atlantic waters.

Stromness: 'and the steps that seek down to the twenty creeled and
salty piers, washed twice a day by cold incoming Atlantic waters.'

# 7
# *Stone*

'The Islands of Stone' they could have been called: there is so much of it everywhere, little fissures in the earth and immense quarries have yielded stone from the time of the first settlement five or six thousand years ago. Men, generation by generation, have turned the stone into things beautiful and useful, grand and simple and good.

They had to use stone. The salty Atlantic winds have seen to it that no trees flourish, except in the little sheltered folds of the hills.

Stone served for the living and the dead. The first Orkney folk must have seen life as a brief flickering flame; few of them lived to be thirty years old, and most of them were probably crippled with rheumatism and respiratory troubles (the same salty dampness that rusts cars nowadays is, at all times, hard on flesh and bone). Death must have seemed to those early fowlers and limpet-gatherers the dark enduring reality: the opposite and complement of their few summers and winters. So to death were reared the best houses; Maeshowe in Stenness is a magnificent burial chamber, the stones of the long entrance corridor so placed that the last light of midwinter enters and splashes briefly one of the tombs: a seed of light sown in the womb of night, winter, death.

A few fields away from Maeshowe are the 'standing stones' that give the parish of Stenness its name. It might never be known what exactly these monoliths are for – astronomy, religion, sacrifice, fertility – argument and speculation have been shuttled back and fore since men decided to dispense with legend; and still we are no nearer the truth. Medieval Orcadians, before the days of reading and counting, wanted to know what the stones were, too. they came to a communal conclusion: they were giants that had been suddenly petrified. Creatures of darkness, the giants had to be home and quarry-fast before the sun got up; otherwise it would go ill with them. Possibly there was some kind of giants' feast at Stenness, between the two lochs, one summer night. Faster and faster the bucket of mead went from mouth to mouth; the bones of mammoth and whale were crunched. A few of the more cautious giants, seeing the first flush in the north-east, thought it was time to be getting off home; and they left the party, singly or in groups. The reckless ones, flushed with drink and fellowship, circled round in yet another moor-dance. Wind piped between the hills – wind stroked the dark glimmering strings of the loch; to that primitive music the reel went round. The sun suddenly looked at them from between two clouds, and that was the end of the Orkney giants. All were turned to stone, even the prudent ones hurrying home to the quarry at Vestrafiold.

The little neolithic stone village of Skara Brae on the west coast of Orkney is a place that touches the heart, because it is on such a human scale: giants and trolls have no place in it; it is a cluster of houses where we can see that people moved and lived and loved: their simple stone artefacts lie everywhere around – dressers, beds, doorposts. A sudden sandstorm, it's said, ended its brief anonymous history. Another westerly gale, thousands of years later, swept the sand blanket away: nineteenth-century laird and crofter and fisherman looked down, awed, at the abode of their remote ancestors, herdsmen and fishermen:

> *As I came home from Sandwick*
> *A star was in the sky.*
> *The northern lights above the hill*
> *Were streaming broad and high.*
> *The tinkers lit their glimmering fires,*
> *Their tents were pitched close by.*
> *But the city of the vanished race*
> *Lay dark and silent in that place.*
> *As I came home from Sandwick*
> *A star was in the sky.*

In a sense we have never fully shrugged off the Stone Age. Within living memory people were sleeping in stone beds. The great millstones that gave the

'The little neolithic stone village of Skara Brae on the west coast of
Orkney . . .'

people their bread and ale have, only lately, lost their fruitful thunders. In spite of concrete and imported wood, the best new houses are still built of local stone; they come out of the quarries strong and beautifully-hued. Stromness will always, to the end of its days, be a stone town like Skara Brae: its score of piers stone feet in the ebb.

It's said that St Magnus once wished to cross the Pentland Firth. There was no boat or boatman handy. He launched a stone from the Caithness shore, and standing on it came safe to Orkney. At a church in South Ronaldsay is the very stone with the saint's foot-marks on it.

But, to pass from medieval miracle, men have written their hearts on the native stone. As remarkable as the stone symbolism of life and death and rebirth in Maeshowe are the runes cut by Norse crusaders on those same walls in the winter of 1151. The fifteen ships sheltered and provisioned in Scapa before taking the sea-road to Narbonne, Jerusalem, Micklegarth, Rome: some of the Viking pilgrims dug their way into the mysterious howe, either out of lust for gold or to prove their courage. On the walls they cut graffiti: INGIBIORG IS THE LOVELIEST OF THE GIRLS and MANY A PROUD WOMAN HAS HAD TO ENTER HERE LOW STOOPING and JERUSALEM-FARERS BROKE IN HERE and HERMUND OF THE HARD AXE CARVED THESE RUNES, and many more; besides cuttings of dragon and walrus.

This writing on stone still goes on, of course. It is a moving experience to wander through any seaside Orkney kirkyard and read the brief biographies of the vanished dead. To wander, and linger, and read, is still to arouse fragrant ghosts.

> *Always, by the shore, kirk and kirkyard.*
> *Legends of men, their carved names*
> *Faced east, into first light, among sea sounds.*

The gravestones are placed to take the risen sun.

So stone fought, over the centuries, its stubborn wars against the new materials: bronze Pictish axes, the silver and gold coins of merchants, iron of plough and clinkered gate and ship, the cans and kettles of wandering tinkers, steel hulls of battleships sunk under Scapa Flow and Marwick Head.

*overleaf* Stone symbols

> The stranger waded ashore.
> His axe-blade
> Bright as the sun, rang once on a stone.
> Then all the stone axes
> Withered in an hour. Then runes
> Were dumb before harp and high voice.

Indeed the metals, when first they came, were looked on as magical materials. An iron stake in the lintel of a house kept trows and evil spirits out. The holy

island, Eynhallow, was plucked out of timelessness by another iron spell. A dark dangerous kind of magic surrounds another element in which Orkney is rich: uranium. The people would rather it lay buried and undisturbed.

Yet stone, the first and the humblest material, has yielded here memorable and beautiful things. Did the planners of St Magnus Cathedral think, while the dream grew in them, of those vast sandstone cliffs that stretch all the way from Westray to Hoy? Did they decide to draw on that awesome strength for their church, so that it would be 'the wonder and glory of all the north'? They knew for sure that sanctity is not all meekness.

'At a church in South Ronaldsay is the very stone with the saint's
foot-marks on it.'

# 8
# *Religion*

We don't know what gods or nature spirits the first Orcadians held in awe and veneration. The seasons turned. In spring the grass came up, the birds returned north, lambs and calves were born. Summer was a good time, brimming with light and fertility. Then came the bronze and russet of autumn. They must have watched the onset of winter with dread. The wick of the sun, so high and potent in summer, was turned lower and weaker. The rain was no longer a filler of springs and a fosterer of grass and herbs; it had a hostile icy edge to it . . . It was likely indeed that time would resume its cycles, and the seed would be waiting under the snow for its vernal summons. But there was no certainty about it: the exquisite equilibrium of the seasons might fail, overbalance from the strong centre. Then the sun would be a cold stone in the sky, and the whole of living things be sheathed in endless frost: grass and well and the lips of young lovers.

The circle of stones at Brodgar: is it a sun symbol? So long as men made appropriate sacrifices there, there would always be a time to love and a time to be born and a time to die for all things – crops and beasts and men. The balance would hold; the slow year-long pulse of the sun in the sky would not desert its treaty with men, symbolised by the circle on the moor. (A circle has no end or beginning.) And yet the moor was dark and barren, a patch of winter between the two lochs. There are minglings of image and of subtle metaphysical dialectic at which we can only dimly guess.

There is no mistaking the midwinter splash of light on the great house of death, Maeshowe. Here the symbolism is daring and triumphant. The torch is plucked from the dying hands of the year: a new time has begun.

'The circle of stones at Brodgar: is it a sun symbol?'

The men of Brodgar and Maeshowe were, as well as builders, seekers into the hidden nature of things.

*Circle of light and darkness, be our sign,*
*We move in shadows.*
*Brodgar has set on the moor a dance of sun.*

*Ring of quern and plough, contain*
*Our tumults of blood.*
*The stars' chaos is caught in a strict rein.*

*Wheel of winter and frost, remove*
*The sweet warm breath.*
Ingibiorg *flowers in stone, all beauty and love.*

All religions, possibly, have their origin in this universal cycle of death, renewal, fulfilment, waning. Nowhere is the drama of light and darkness enacted with such starkness as in the north.

The priest-kings and worshippers of the early Orkney tribes vanished. The Norsemen who first plundered and then settled had their own pantheon: of whom the most appealing by far is Balder the Beautiful, the god of light. Word came at last of a doom upon Balder: he must die soon. But who or what would want to do an injury to this darling of the gods? His mother set out on a painful journey through the earth. She wrung promises from every living thing, plant and animal and bird, earth and sea and sky, that they would never hurt Balder. At last, her mission accomplished, she turned her steps homeward. True, there was one plant at the wintry edge of the world, far far away, called mistletoe, that she hadn't bothered to visit. It was a pale sickly growth – inconceivable that it could ever harm the radiant immortal body of Balder ... But Loki, the mischief-maker, contrived one day of high sport in Asgard to put a spear made of mistletoe into the hand of a blind god. All the gods, to reassure Balder that he was invulnerable and immortal, had set him in the centre of a ring and were deluging his brightness with all kinds of missile. The blind god, in order to do honour to the one they all loved so much, flung the mistletoe: it pierced Balder's heart, and he died.

But Balder returns each spring, and the days of darkness and mistletoe and ice are forgotten. A green wave goes over the world, again and again.

The plot is the same; only the masks and the scenes are different. We may be sure the Picts, and the tribes before them, had their own forgotten stories to explain winter and summer, death and harvest, light and darkness.

It is but one step from those deeply ingrained beliefs to the knowledge of good and evil. Man perhaps becomes increasingly aware of himself as an individual: the tides of light and darkness mesh in his own heart; that is all eventually that need concern him, what D. H. Lawrence called disparagingly 'the isolate salvation of the single soul'. Yet to ignore the unity of the tribe, the nation, the race, is to go against the grain of the human spirit from the beginning. We are all indissolubly involved in each other and in the whole totality of human kind, dead and unborn, from the beginning to an unforeseeable end. 'No man is an island.'

The first Christians were there already, Celtic monks and missionaries: they went with mild mouths and dove-shaped hands among the doom-ridden Norsemen of Orkney; and no doubt many a monk who had been spirit-kindled by Columba and Ninian in the west had their martyrdom sealed by axe and fire.

Time passed: Orkney was converted to Christianity in a singular yet typical fashion. Earl Sigurd, on shipboard at Osmundwall off the island of Hoy, had an unexpected sea visit from his liege-lord King Olaf of Norway. The king said, 'Either you consent to be baptised now, or every man of you will be killed.' So Sigurd and his men became reluctant Christians there and then. To see that there would be no backsliding, King Olaf took Earl Sigurd's son, a boy called Hundi, back with him to Norway. Hundi died there in a short time. Sigurd reverted to the gods of his fathers; he died fighting against the Christian High King of Ireland, Brian Boru, at Clontarf in Ireland.

In spite of Earl Sigurd's relapse, Christianity had taken root, and it spread rapidly. It was a great-grandson of the same fate-ridden Sigurd who gave the most extreme and dramatic witness to Christianity in the north.

On Easter Monday, 1117, two men confronted each other in the island of Egilsay: Hakon Paulsson and Magnus Erlendsson. These men, cousins, were joint earls of Orkney. Double rule, or even treble rule, had been a commonplace in the history of the earldom. It suited the purposes of the king of Norway, the overlord; a divided earldom was never in danger of asserting itself as a strong

St Magnus Church, Egilsay: 'On Easter Monday, 1117, two men
confronted each other in the island of Egilsay: Hakon Paulsson and
Magnus Erlendsson.'

semi-independent entity. But the consequences, generation after generation, for the commons of Orkney were woeful and bitter: taxmen everywhere, soldiers in the corn-fields, a burning of mill and homestead.

Hakon and Magnus had come together to heal the always-opening wound. It was to have been a peace-meeting. Magnus came, the dove in his hand. Hakon came with a gang of armed ruffians. An execution was carried out: Lifolf, Earl Hakon's cook, drove the axe into Magnus's forehead, weeping as he did so.

And that was that. With a single stroke Hakon had united the earldom. Politically it had been a wise – indeed the *only* – thing to do. Earl Hakon proved himself afterwards to be an able, strong, and generous governor, 'so that (the *Saga* says) the Orkneymen desired to have no other earl but him . . .'

But strange things were happening in secret northern places. People with harelips and black coughs and scabs and deranged minds and quenched eyes began to go, or to be led, to the murdered earl's tomb in Birsay. They crossed the ebb to the steep green island where the church was, carrying their candles and offerings, and many of them were cured. The cult of Magnus spread rapidly all over the north; the common people canonised the slain earl years before the church called him Magnus Martyr.

Now the bones – the cleft skull and all – lie in a pillar of the red Cathedral in Kirkwall that bears his name.

The man who ordered the building of St Magnus Cathedral was Magnus's nephew, Earl Rognvald Kolson, one of the most attractive figures in *Orkneyinga Saga*. Besides the great minster at the heart of Orkney, Earl Rognvald ordered the building of a fine ship in Norway, gold inlaid, with benches for seventy rowers. This was to be the principal ship of a fleet of fifteen, bound on a pilgrimage to Jerusalem: a holy voyage. With Earl Rognvald sailed the Bishop of Orkney, William the Old, and many of the finest young men from Scandinavia and the islands. It turned out to be no voyage of unsullied piety: they mingled with their eternal yearnings such immediate necessites as war, love, and piracy. But in the end, bearing palm branches, they stood among the bright stones of Jerusalem.

After his brutal death in Caithness Rognvald – scholar, pilgrim, chess-player, poet – was called saint also.

Orcadians have never been zealots in religion. The Reformation, when it

Father Spencer with congregation at the Italian Chapel. 'Now,
once a month each summer, a mass is said there.'

came in the mid-sixteenth century, seems to have been a quiet affair, carried out in some council chamber rather than in the burning hearts of men. At any rate, the Cathedral survived the change. Two centuries later, Orkney peasants were still leaving votive offerings in the ruins of the old chapels that were everywhere in the islands: occasion of many a thunderous sermon from eighteenth-century pulpits.

Many of those Presbyterian ministers were extraordinary men: classicists like Rev William Clouston of Stromness, naturalists like Rev George Low of Birsay and Dr Charles Clouston of Sandwick, eccentrics like Rev John Gerard of South Ronaldsay (he was a man of massive common sense and humour, but with a streak of melancholy).

In the nineteenth century Orkney must have been black with ministers; secession after secession from the established Church of Scotland meant that some parishes and islands had as many as three ministers at one time. Nowadays the number of clergymen is much what it was two centuries ago: ecumenism is all, these days.

There is one building in a little uninhabited island that tourists flock to by the thousand each summer. Italian prisoners of war helped with the construction of the huge Churchill barriers that link five islands together across the vulnerable east side of Scapa Flow. The Italian soldiers stayed on a bleak islet called Lamb Holm. Nothing on earth could have been more different from the vales of Tuscany and the little medieval towns of home, with winepress, olives, and bell-tower. Perhaps as much out of homesickness as of religious impulse they began to build, from two nissen huts and any scrap of metal and wood they could lay hands on, a little church; and they painted and decorated it inside in the Mediterranean tradition. (Earl Rognvald and his pilgrims would have known at once what the Italian soldiers were doing.) For a time after the war the little chapel was threatened with rot and rust. In the end it was saved by local people who saw that this was a beautiful place, and also perhaps a symbol of reconciliation and peace. The chapel was restored by one of the original builders, Domenico Chiochetti. Now, once a month each summer, a mass is said there.

# 9
# *Occupations*

That huge gas flare at the centre of Scapa Flow, the blazon that illumines Orkney's night sky, might well stand as a sign of the new industrial age, 'things to come'. Between the oil wells under the North Sea and the tanks of Flotta stretch, unseen, the vast veins and arteries of the new technology. Tankers bigger than some of the islands come and go between Scapa Flow and the refineries and oil-hungry nations near and remote.

The Orcadians take it with a strange casualness, as if nothing on earth or undersea really surprised them. They have, of course, been conditioned for three generations or so; ever since, on a late summer night in 1914, the people of Hoy saw the battleships of Britain steaming silently into Scapa Flow ... The pulse has never really been silent since. A major industry between the wars was the salvaging of the self-sunk German Fleet from those same gray depths. That work was still going on when World War Two broke out. At once Orkney was invaded by regiments and battalions and squadrons of soldiers and airmen. The navy returned, anxiously; for now Scapa Flow was well within the radius of air attack, and, as it proved, of deadly submarine attack – the war was only a few weeks old when Prien's torpedoes sank the *Royal Oak*.

Ruins of army encampments lie everywhere – fighter aerodromes in the centre of the fertile West Mainland – naval piers and concealed storage tanks in the island of Hoy: Orkney has been inured to huge influxes of men and money, and to the shapes of the machine age. The ugly concrete scars of 1939–45 still disfigure our countryside here and there. What could be more incongruous than the magnificent coastline of Yesnaby scabbed with the remnants of a naval gunnery range? The trouble with modern building materials is that time sours and stains them; whereas the local stone used for six thousand years and more weathers to beauty and aptness, as if buildings and landscape were made for each other.

Compared to the convulsion of 1914 and 1939, the oil industry is a smallish affair, that seems unlikely, in the long run, to make a large dent on the history and ecology of the islands.

What Orcadians fear – though they rarely speak about it – is that there might well be an accidental oil spillage that would pollute our coast lines from North Ronaldsay to Stroma. The local fishermen, of course, fear for their livelihood. But conservationists and those concerned with the natural environment – Orkney has plenty of such guardians – are keeping vigilant eyes on the situation.

'Things to come' may appear in more ominous disguises. It is known that there are deposits of uranium ore in Orkney, especially in a thick belt stretching from the north end of Stromness to Yesnaby. Recently the South of Scotland Electricity Board asked for permission to do some test borings. The move provoked immediate and spontaneous outcry. Petitions of protest were starred with thousands of signatures; the BBC and ITV sent up reporters and television teams; there was a solemn winter morning march along the streets of Kirkwall, in which Orcadians of all ages took part, to hand in the petitions at the offices of the Islands Council.

This popular protest was strange in a way, coming from a people that dislikes demonstration and outward flourishes. In one mood, indeed, the Orcadians seem to be oversold on the idea of progress and the exploitation of their own natural resources. They have never been averse to the idea of surpluses of money spilling over into the local economy... The recent world-wounds of Hiroshima and Nagasaki are still vivid in the memory; and even the peaceful use of uranium seems to them fraught with dangers unknown before to humanity, that look as if they might take decades or centuries to resolve... In addition, Orcadians have come to have a deep love of the physical appearance of their islands; the thought of possible open-cast mining in a lovely region of Orkney deeply disturbs them. The Geiger counter, pulsing madly near Cairston Mill – it was shown on our TV screens – might have excited Orcadians in other circumstances; it seemed an ominous symbol in the winter of 1977.

There is another side to the uranium issue, which physicists and geologists and politicians will argue. But a people's deep instinctive urges ought never to be discounted. The land is theirs, after all, and the earth-wisdom that comes from many generations of work on it.

From the beginning of June until the end of September, each year in increasing numbers, Orkney is thronged with tourists. They come by air and sea; cars by the thousand are ferried across the Pentland Firth on the drive-on M V *St Ola*. Orkney in high summer is like a shaken ant-hill. What is intriguing is that, unlike ants, our summer-time tourists have an almost infinite variety. In the 1930s, the tourists seemed to consist mainly of elderly genteel people, and a few eccentrics. Ladies would set up easels before Melvin Place or Flaws' pier in Stromness and discreetly apply water-colour splashes; gentlemen would roam the hillsides with binoculars and bird-books. The nature-lovers still come, amateur archaeologists, those in search of unspoilt sources; and there is, on the whole, adequate hotel and bed-and-breakfast accommodation for them. But, increasingly, it is the younger tourists who swarm in, from all over Europe and beyond; they live, for the most part, in hostels and tents; and they stir some freshness, adventure, excitement into our quiet round. The Orcadians, being a curious and friendly people, get on well with those careless invaders; who, apart from all else, deposit each year another thin layer of gold on the island economy.

The inherent wealth of the soil goes into the famous products of two distilleries in Kirkwall – Highland Park and Scapa. Their malt whiskies are becoming increasingly popular everywhere; and their rare tinctures enrich other famous blended whiskies.

Two creameries, in Kirkwall and Birsay, produce the popular 'Claymore' butter and cheese, and 'Swannay' cheese. In this farm and that, of course, the keeper of the hearth still makes her own distinctive cheese, butter, bannocks, ale, jam.

Boat-building has of course been an island craft for many generations.

Thirled to boat-building is the oldest industry of all – fishing – the hunt through the sea for the gray and silver legions; nets let down for the armoured ocean-bed samurai – lobster and crab. Fishing has always been a precarious occupation, and always will be. Hardly a year passes without young men being lost somewhere along the Orkney coast.

The Duncan brothers of Duncans' yard in Burray. Their boat-
building business goes back five generations!

*Houses went blind*
*Up one steep close, for a*
*Grief by the shrouded nets.*

Besides the danger of his trade, the fisherman of only a generation ago was poorly rewarded. In the 1920s the inshore fishermen, working the lines from small boats, afterwards would sell their haddocks at threepence a pound from hand-barrows along the streets of Stromness.

Since the setting-up of the Orkney Fishermen's Society the whole outlook has changed in the fishermen's favour: live lobster, frozen crab and scallop, have found eager markets as far away as London, Paris, Amsterdam, Copenhagen. At present there are crab processing factories in Stromness, Westray, Rousay. The fishing future is brighter than it has ever been; except in the great nineteenth-century herring harvests that dazzled and overwhelmed and left at last a great desolation behind.

In Stromness there is a prosperous toffee factory – Robertson's Orkney fudge, like Highland Park whisky, and live lobsters out of Hoy Sound, is enjoyed all over the world.

Beautifully designed jewellery, with local motifs, is created in two separate workshops in Kirkwall. There are, of course, knitwear firms. Potteries have recently been set up in country districts, and the products are full of imagination and fine craft: a home-brew set, consisting of a jug and half dozen mugs, seen recently in Tormiston Mill, had the true Orkney countryside grained into it. New ventures burgeon everywhere, in unlikely places.

So, modern Orkney is a pattern of industries old and new; and no one can say what the kaleidoscope will show at the next shaking.

Whatever the future holds, it seems likely that the last Orcadians, like the first, will be a pastoral agricultural fishing people. Without the earth-worker who has often been despised in the past by ignorant urban people on account of the 'dust and dung' he has to work among – without the farmer, no civilisation past or future is conceivable. Behind symphonies, great art and literature, politics and philosophy and law, is the cornstalk.

Nowadays agriculture in Orkney is highly mechanised; it was a curious phenomenon, a century ago, that Orcadians took to the machine so fervently – almost as if they had been waiting for its advent patiently for a long time. 'How

87

Willie Sinclair: '. . . live lobsters out of Hoy Sound, [are] enjoyed
all over the world.'

things work' has always fascinated the Orkneyman. Toil on croft and farm, in the early nineteenth century and before, must have been hard and anxious and arduous... Yet it is a moving experience to wander round a place of ruined crofts, like Rackwick in Hoy, and see the ploughs slowly rusting at gable-end, and the quernstones that ground the people's oats set up against the wall as ornaments; and the kiln at Crowsnest a slow dilapidation.

There was an order and ceremony there that is lost forever.

To look much further back, to the very beginning. The first Orkneymen only fished perhaps in the rock pools for limpet, whelk, mussel. In a lucky time, a whale might blunder ashore. We may imagine a time when there was famine even in the ebb. It is in such seasons of peril that, suddenly, a single imagination is quickened. A young man, anxious and hungry, scratched on stone the curve of a boat, the curve of an oar, the curve of a sail: next winter the doors of Skara Brae were hung with Atlantic fish... Image begets image. Perhaps it was not so long after, that a herdsman of the people, watching his sheep at their grazing, said, wonderingly, 'Why shouldn't the earth give nourishment to men as well as to beasts?' The answer to that question were the curves of plough, sickle, quern.

So the crofter-fisherman came with his signs; and his coming transformed society beyond recognition.

Whatever 'things to come' happen, may a saving imagination never fail us.

# 10
# *War*
====

Elsewhere in this book, mention has been made of Orkney's 'golden age' – the time of the Norse earls, with their great hospitable halls and their beautiful ships and their retinues of poets. But even the best of times – the last years of Earl Thorfinn and the wise firm rule of Earl Hakon the saint-killer – were threatened with violence from beyond the horizon and laced red with private feud and murder. The only golden age for the peasant and his family was a year when the corn came up thick and burnished for the sickles of peace. The peasant knew, more vividly than those in power, how precarious life is: the armed horseman rides through his green corn, he is likely to be dragged from his hearth if the island chief is short of an oarsman for his spring pirate-voyage.

Raid, siege, battle go, a fatal undersong, through the history of the islands. Here and there, along sea coast or at loch-side are the remnants of brochs. These are marvellously-constructed primitive keeps or castles, and almost impregnable. The two concentric walls of a broch are bound together by a stone circling stair inside; any besieger rash enough to sit outside would be instantly and incessantly deluged with stone, arrow, fire, ordure. Any besieger hoping to starve the garrison into surrender needed long patience: for inside the broch would be food enough to last for as long as was necessary, and, at the centre, a well of ever-brimming water. The heart of the besieger might well quail, looking day after day (from a respectable distance) at the solid blank dangerous stone behive.

But the broch builders themselves must have put the yoke on an earlier people: it has been suggested that the idea of trows came from those conquered original folk whom they drove into the interior hills and marshes, but who ventured out by night with noose and knife to take vengeance on the Celtic usurpers. Nobody knows how many waves of conquest went over the islands from the time of the first settlers. Certainly much that was rare and beautiful must have been destroyed in those anonymous centuries.

The Norsemen are still looked on as the greatest and most colourful in all the long procession of islanders, from stone-age men to Scots, and indeed they had many admirable qualities: stoicism, humour, resource, a rough-and-ready code of law, a taste for narrative, a fine contempt of death. But they in their turn destroyed what must have been a well-integrated artistic society.

*The first ones came. They had no wings on their helmets. They were gaunt and sea-gray. They offered bits of bronze. The people of the island gave them bread and milk. They turned their lean ship round.*

*The next ones, twenty years later, came with hides, silver and walrus ivory. An axe glinted here and there. They asked if there was land for sale. One of the sailors pointed to a dark girl.*

*They dribbled in, over a decade: by shipwreck or design or exile. Islanders set a shivering one before the peat-fire.*

*They came at last in a huge bronze wave. They had nothing to trade. They possessed the wells, the barns, the glebes. They made songs in praise of wolf and hawk. They herded together the girls with black hair.*

*These are our heroes, the lauded ones. Praise rather the first breakers of the earth, the hewers of stones, the subtle ones who divined water and opened wells. It is their quiet voices that will end the story.*

The Norse centuries in Orkney were stimulating as flung spindrift, but that time can also be looked at in another way. An Icelandic poet saw the marvellous tapestry as a web of ghastliness and insane rage, into which the hearts and entrails of the great warriors were gathered.

> *The warp is stretched*
> *For warriors' death.*
> *The weft in the loom*
> *Drips with blood.*

*The battle darkens.*
*Under our fingers*
*The tapestry grows,*
*Red as heart's blood,*
*Blue as corpses,*
*The web of battle.*

*What is this woof?*
*The guts of men,*
*The weights on the warp*
*Their slaughtered heads . . .*
*With swords for shuttles*
*The war-web we weave,*
*Valkyries weaving*
*The web of victory . . .*

Many Orkneymen followed their earl, Sigurd, to the dynastic battle fought on
Good Friday, 1014, at Clontarf in Ireland.

*Sigurd is the name of our earl.*
*His mother the witch*
*Wove our black banner. The raven*
*Streams and flaps above the host.*
*Who bears that bird of victory*
*Drinks tonight in dark halls.*
*Now Sigurd, alone,*
*Offers the raven to a sackcloth sun.*

*I forget the name of the saint*
*That saved my grandfather*
*Under the walls of Paris one summer.*
*Whatever your name is, white one,*
*I am grandson*
*To old Olaf, that you kept from torrents of*
*lead and tar,*

92

*One day in a French siege.*
*I will light candles for you.*

*I bought the horse in Dublin.*
*Seven times*
*It reared against horn and shield wall.*
*Now the horse is hide and bone,*
*I am walking back to the town.*
*At the river mouth*
*The proud Minch-trampler is moored.*

*Coming to Ireland*
*We stopped first at Barra.*
*A cold week, snow in the ale.*

*Coming to Ireland*
*About some royal mix-up or other,*
*We stopped next at Man.*
*Coming to Ireland*
*We have stopped at this noisy fairground.*
*There seems to be no road out of it.*

*I drank thick ale in Galloway.*
*Battles, blood, wall-breaching —*
*Bravely I boasted!*
*Now the glory is come*
*There is no ditch anywhere*
*I would not creep into,*
*Sharing a mushroom with tramp or slut.*

The most fascinating insight into the complex nature of those Norse Orkney-men is provided by the 'Jerusalem-farers' chapters in *Orkneyinga Saga*. The fifteen ships of Earl Rognvald Kolson set out on a crusade – 'pilgrimage' would be a more accurate description, since there were no infidels to fight at that particular time (1151–54). This God-faring may be seen as an act of penance done on behalf of an entire people, to redeem a savage history, to turn over the page scarred with red and write words of grace on the new white parchment.

93

But pirates don't become saints overnight. Between Scapa and the domes of Jerusalem the cold-eyed seamen dallied for months in the port of Narbonne, and the earl fell in love, in the courtly fashion of the time, with the countess Ermengarde. His mouth brimmed with skaldic verse that must have sounded barbarous in the ear of a girl attuned to the bird-notes and fragrances and exquisite shapes of Provençal verse.

They broke at last out of the honeyed web of Narbonne, and came half-starved to a port in Galicia. The townsfolk refused to open their stores to them, for, said they, they had little to give – the Castle on the hill seized all the grapes and olives and fish that they had reaped by their labour. In the cold and hunger of mid-winter the pilgrims reduced the Castle to a smoking ruin; and, judging by the *Saga*, they did their old pagan work with style and relish.

With style and relish, too, a few months later, they surrounded and captured and burned a Moslem merchant-ship, a large 'dromond'. Out of the side of the flaming ship flowed, like honey, streams of molten gold. The black captain said he would rather the sea had his treasure than the Vikings. His wit and courage saved him. The pilgrims set him ashore safe at his own port.

At every landfall they fought and got drunk and were the kind of men they had always been.

*A hundred swords were broken that voyage.*
*Prayer on a hundred white wings*
*Rose every morning. The Mediterranean*
*Was richer by a hundred love songs.*

Into the tapestry of blood and guts were gathered all the same, and for the first time, rose and dove and palm-branch.

King Hakon of Norway with a great fleet arrived in Orkney in 1263. His mission was to reassert Norway's sovereignty over those parts of Scotland that had for so long been within the circle of Norwegian influence. Slowly, that Scandinavian influence had been eroding as Scotland became ever more aware of itself as a nation. King Hakon's fleet sailed down the west coast. A storm threw some of his ships against the coast, near Largs. Round those ships the battle was fought, without any clear-cut decision. But the eye of history saw it as a Scottish victory, for the old snow king sailed north again; and that was the last time a Norse king threatened Scotland. In Orkney the king sickened. As death approached the priests read to him from the Latin scriptures. Later, in the Bishop's Palace where he lay, he asked for the sagas of his ancestors to be read to him. His body lay that winter in St Magnus Cathedral.

Eventually not only the Western Isles but Orkney and Shetland became part of Scotland, in fulfilment of the marriage contract between King James III of Scotland and a Danish princess. The islands were pledged for a huge sum of money, which in fact was never paid. For the Norn-speaking Orkney people it must have been a difficult time. New alien laws threatened their ancient udal tenures. Increasingly Scotsmen were brought into positions of power. Orcadians remembered the authority and influence that Orkney had once held in the counsels of the north; now it was only a remote province of Scotland, open for any Scottish adventurer or sycophant to strip and despoil. Eventually it came to armed rebellion. King James V sent from Caithness, under the command of Lord William St Clair, a royal punitive force. At a place called Summerdale, on the borders of Orphir and Stenness, the Orkney rebels swarmed out of the hills and cut the Caithness army to pieces. Only one Orkney boy was killed, and that by his own mother; he had stripped the uniform from a dead Caithness soldier and was returning home under the first stars; the mother, having heard all day the thunder of battle among the hills, assumed that the royal army had been victorious, and that her son was probably wounded to death or hanged; she filled a long stocking with stones and struck the oncoming green-clad figure again and again until he was dead.

Later, King James visited Orkney, and his presence patched up a peace that was never seriously threatened again.

One troop of young Orkneymen followed Montrose in his last campaign against Cromwell and the Parliament. At Carbisdale in the Highlands they were crushed by well-armed professional troops; it's said that not one found his way back to Orkney.

Only the Orkney lairds showed any enthusiasm for the Jacobite Rebellion of 1745. After Culloden, many of them spent miserable months hiding in a cave in Westray, still known as Gentlemen's Ha'.

The long wars of the eighteenth century brought much shipping and wealth into Orkney, especially to the growing town of Stromness. The later Napoleonic wars brought terror to many an Orkney croft. The great men-of-war were constantly in need of seamen. In Orkney, as in every other maritime place, the 'press-gang' were busy. If young men did not volunteer for the offered bounty money, they were seized in the fields and fishing-nousts. Many of them never saw the islands again. There is a treasury of press-gang stories, in which a constant theme is the outwitting of the press-gang by sweethearts and mothers of the young men sought.

French and American privateers swarmed everywhere in those days and were a constant menace to British merchant ships. The island of Hoy in Orkney has its Martello defensive towers, but it seems they never uttered thunder and flame. (Of all the hundreds of Martello towers, the only one to gain fame is the one James Joyce lived in at Sandymount, Dublin, in 1904.)

In 1914 the main naval base of the British Navy was Scapa Flow, the wide stretch of sea enclosed by the southern Mainland shore and the south islands of Orkney, yet giving easy access to the Atlantic and the North Sea. Out of Scapa Flow the *Hampshire* sailed one stormy June day in 1916, carrying Lord Kitchener on his way to Russia for military talks. Off Marwick Head in Birsay the warship struck a mine and went down. Only a handful of men survived out of eight or nine hundred. Kitchener with his cold 'your-country-needs-you' eye was one with pearl and coral.

Out of Scapa Flow also sailed the British Fleet to challenge the German Grand Fleet at Jutland in 1916 – the battle that was claimed as a victory by both sides.

In Scapa Flow in June 1919 the same surrendered German Grand Fleet committed suicide. At a given signal the cocks were opened and one by one the huge ships heeled over. The intricate and technically difficult salvage of them was, between the two wars, a major industry in Orkney; the steel of the German warships was of the highest quality.

Again, in 1939, the British Navy sought the security of Scapa Flow. A few weeks after the war started a daring U-boat commander, Günther Prien, entered Scapa Flow through Water Sound and drove torpedoes into HMS *Royal Oak* lying under the sea-cliffs of Holm. Again hundreds of young sailors were killed. A buoy marks the place where the great ship and her crew have their sea burial. Prien went home to a hero's welcome, and received the Iron Cross

'The island of Hoy in Orkney has its Martello defensive towers, but
it seems they never uttered thunder and flame.'

*overleaf* Barriers and Blockships

from Hitler himself. Later he went down with his U-boat.

For the first time for centuries Orkney was actually in the front line of war: in the dark of the moon squadrons of German bombers probed the defences of Scapa Flow again and again. The circle of seeking searchlights, the vivid pandemonium of the anti-aircraft guns, the faint undulant drone of the German bombers made high dangerous drama for the Orcadians of 1940 and 1941. Over the little hamlet of Brig-o-Waithe, between the sea and the Loch of Stenness, a fleeing bomber scattered its incendiaries. A villager standing in his doorway was killed, others were injured – they were the first British civilian casualties of the war.

In those days Orkney was crammed with garrison troops. They outnumbered the island folk probably by three to one. In the centre of the main island were two fighter aerodromes, at Skeabrae and Twatt. So far from there being any friction between servicemen and islanders, there was such harmony throughout

those five years that many ex-soldiers and airmen return this summer or that; as in the First World War, too, there were scores of marriages between servicemen and Orkney girls, and as often as not they settled in the islands, and begot a new generation of Orcadians.

All that massive expenditure of energy and money was for the defence of Scapa Flow. There is not very much to show for it now. But one piece of defence has, over the years, become an indispensable feature of Orkney: the Churchill barriers built, after Prien and the *Royal Oak*, to seal the eastern gates into Scapa Flow.

The scarlet threads of war are plentiful in the history of Orkney. What Orcadians hope now is that the tapestry will grow with peaceful natural greens and blues; another war would put an end forever to the threads and the loom and the patient weaving hands.

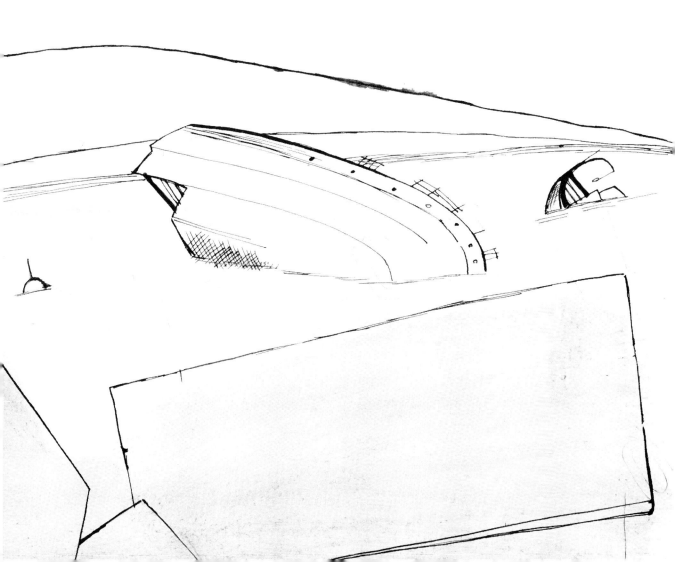

# I I
# *Song and Sign*

Orkney has more artists, writers, musicians than most other small communities.

Yet, when I was young, there was little sign of it. Not that we cared: football and reading comics were nearest to our hearts.

We knew, vaguely, that there was a Kirkwall-born artist, Stanley Cursiter, who was director of the National Gallery in Edinburgh, and a painter himself. We knew the name of a writer called Eric Linklater whose novels slightly shocked the Orkney ladies who read Ethel M. Dell and Annie S. Swan from the Library.

We had never heard of Edwin Muir.

A few lady tourists used to set up easels at Stromness street corners in summer and paint water-colours. How strange! – What could they see in our light-of-common-day place worth painting?

Here and there, on the walls of a 'better-class' house, you might see the engravings of the Daniells, made in the early nineteenth century, of Orkney scenes. There was even one of Stromness.

Of music: nothing. The Balfour collection of old Orkney melodies was rarely opened. In a farm here and there there were fiddlers who played the traditional Scottish reels.

But the local Library had one boys' book called *Pilots of Pomona*, by Robert Leighton, and that was about a boy in Stromness too. (Robert Leighton was not himself an Orcadian.) A few of us read *Pilots of Pomona* with joy. Apart from the opening scene – the young hero plays truant – I remember nothing. *The Fight at Summerdale, The Boys of Hamnavoe*, both by John Gunn: we must have read them too. My father used to tell how John Gunn, a small farmer's

Marian Ashburn sketching at West-shore: 'Orkney has more
artists, writers, musicians than most other small communities.'

son, went to school in Stromness on bare feet, a peat under his arm to help keep the school fire going. My father liked stories like that, about poor boys who 'got on in the world'. One of the few books in our house was *From Log Cabin to White House*, about some nineteenth-century American President. In school, at home, on the streets, we drew it in with every breath – 'You are here to better yourself'... That meant, for the sons of crofters, labourers, and fishermen, that eventually, if they worked hard at their lessons, they might get a job in a lawyer's office, or as a bank clerk. Even to work behind a counter in a shop was better (the unspoken solicitation went) than following a plough or catching fish.

I was never taken in by this philosophy. That bleak foolish unlovely flower of self-improvement is dust now, fortunately.

We never got to know about the *Orkneyinga Saga* and the treasures of medieval narrative it contained.

Orkney seemed, then, in the first half of the twentieth century, a cultural desert. Not that we twelve-year-olds cared; so long as there was a football match coming off between Stromness Athletic and one of the three Kirkwall teams. All the joy and rapture of life lay in such encounters. The young men in the local football team were our Achilles and Agamemnon and Patroclus. When they defeated Kirkwall Hotspur, the walls of Troy were breached!

In a book like this, nobody wants a learned thesis on modern Orkney culture. Let these essays gather dust on shelves. What I'd like to do is to provide a few thumb-nail sketches of some artists I've known.

Who better to begin with than Ian MacInnes, who sat in the same class-room with me for twelve years or so? In his teens he began to sketch local people. He had the gift early of catching an astonishing likeness, and his sitters were not aware that there was an artist among them, nor that a caricature of this townsman or that would soon appear in the *Orkney Herald*, every Tuesday. When that paper was opened, there was great merriment along the street. Ian MacInnes is now a fine portrait painter, and celebrates, in canvas after canvas, the power and beauty of the Atlantic gnawing at the coast of Yesnaby.

And once he left his easel and colour-box on the cliff-top at Yesnaby, and went down to a ledge to make a quick sketch. The poet Robert Rendall came past, saw the artist's paraphernalia but not the artist, and concluded that he

'... the power and the beauty of the Atlantic gnawing at the coast of Yesnaby.'

might have 'gone afore the face' (that is, fallen over the cliff). How relieved he was, presently, to see Ian MacInnes climbing up with his sketch pad in his hand. They were great friends, Robert Rendall and Ian MacInnes, though in outlook and opinion they were opposite in almost every way.

Robert Rendall was a draper, profoundly deaf, and a lyric poet of high excellence. That he wrote in the Orkney dialect keeps him from having a nationwide fame. He found his purest inspiration in the Greek Anthology. He infused those lyrics with northern magic. Besides poetry, Robert Rendall was a conchologist of renown, and he wrote books of theology. The Birsay shore, not the Kirkwall draper shop, was his place. His fine spirit quested among the rockpools and the shells and algae. He could laugh with delight, like a boy.

Eric Linklater we saw sometimes in summer, sailing his boat *Skua* in the Stromness regatta, or playing golf; and at the outset of war going to his Royal Engineers office in Alfred Street, the major's crown on his shoulder. The first reading of his novels *Whitemaa's Saga* and *Magnus Merriman* were pure joy to our opening minds. We were beginning to know that our islands were beautiful and rich in history – Eric Linklater first charted that richness and beauty for us, like an explorer returned. I only managed to speak to him once, a year or two before his death, in a house beside the Loch of Harray that he describes so magically in the opening page of his first autobiography.

The name of Edwin Muir kept appearing, in magazines and books. But the poetry was obscure; and this islander had moved out of Orkney early, and was living here and there in Europe and England. Then one war-time day I took down a copy of a book called *The Story and the Fable* from the town Library shelves: the timeless world of an island infancy came off the pages, sweet and pure as clover and shells.

After the war, Stanley Cursiter came home to Orkney, and restored a boat-building yard near Hamnavoe for his house and studio. A tall erect handsome smiling man, he could be seen most days on the street. He presented the town with a magnificent sea-and-cliffscape of Yesnaby, called 'Linklater and Greig' after the fishermen whose boat is coming in on the Atlantic surge ...

In a Kirkwall bookshop one day I spoke to a new assistant, a young bespectacled man called Ernest Marwick. Soon we were abroad on 'the foam of perilous seas' – poetry. Did I write verse, he wanted to know. He was compiling *An Anthology of Orkney Verse*, and was eager to have modern Orkney poets represented. When the book appeared, in 1949, it was no frail collection of regional verse: it was a work of penetrating scholarship that revealed the richness of medieval poetry, in Norse and Scots, that had been made in Orkney. The scholar in him was never at odds with the artist; Ernest was poet, painter, photographer himself. He died, tragically, in a car accident, leaving behind a rich archive of island history and lore: most of it still unpublished. His house in Kirkwall, 'Westermill', was a meeting-place for writers and lovers of literature. And it overflowed with goodness and hospitality. His wife, Janette, was herself a very delightful woman . . .

I have spent many happy evenings at the fireside of Bessie Grieve and her husband James in Harray. She is a story-teller, poet, and nature-lover, and she brews magical ale. In the Grieves' little house on the moor I met her father, also a poet: John Skea, farmer, of Shapinsay. The spell of poetry was on him still in his old age: I will never forget him reciting the *Lays of Ancient Rome* and Francis Thompson's poem about a legendary Lancashire cricket team: 'O my Hornby and my Barlow long ago!' . . . John Skea's own sonnets were beautifully turned.

In North Ronaldsay lives Ian Scott, farmer and painter and sculptor. On the shore of the Loch of Skaill lives Margaret Tait, film-maker. Down an old pier in Stromness lives Gunnie Moberg, photographer. There are artists, print-makers, makers of musical instruments, potters, tapestry-makers, everywhere in the islands. Perhaps the characteristic common to all of them is modesty. They have never been tutored in how to sell themselves. But time will sift and save the gold.

One day in Stromness I met Edwin and Willa Muir at last. After a pleasant conversation, over afternoon tea in the hotel, I was enrolled as a student at Newbattle, near Edinburgh, where Muir was Warden. By this time, having read 'The Voyage' and 'The Labyrinth', I knew I was talking to the greatest poet Orkney had put forth since the anonymous ballad-men. I have written elsewhere, and at length, of the stimulus and encouragement this shy modest man gave me. Perhaps the most memorable thing about that first meeting was the archaic music of his voice. After decades of absence – in Glasgow, living here and there in Europe and England and Scotland – he kept still the tone and rhythm of island speech. It was the clue, perhaps, that led him out of the labyrinth in which he was lost for so long: the man had not forgotten the child, and the childhood that was the master-light of all his seeing.

One day, in the summer of 1946, I saw Rackwick in Hoy for the first time. We drove in a farmer's lorry between dark hills, and suddenly a sea valley was there, between immense red cliffs. I had not thought there could be a place so beautiful. It seemed like 'the island-valley of Avilion' where King Arthur was taken to heal him of his grievous wound. The valley was touched with sadness. One by one the little crofts were falling into ruins. There were a few elderly people left, one working farm, and a forlorn scattering of children where once there had been a throng. A burn sang down from the hills and lost itself among the huge round many-coloured boulders of the shore. But the shore, like the tilth and pasture, was empty of the fishing boats that had once been the valley's chief food-gatherers.

That first glimpse of Rackwick had haunted my imagination ever since. I wrote, later, an entire book of poems about it, *Fishermen with Ploughs*. I tried, through the prism of art – which is different from history – to see life in Rackwick from the time of the first settlers on into a future where progress and science have done their utmost and left the lonely and beautiful places of earth to decay.

Rackwick began to attract artists soon afterwards. Sylvia Wishart made habitable a crofthouse that was quickly withering, and painted Rackwick in all weathers. I remember a day in late winter when unexpected snow, shower after shower, slowly covered the valley with an immaculate cloak. Sylvia sat in the doorway of a broken croft and her brush went singing across the canvas, a blue and silver composition. In bad weather, she painted again and again the lamp in the window of North-house, with the immense red cliffs standing out in the bay.

Ian MacInnes bought a house, Noust, down at the shore; the patterns of sea and sky and cliff delighted him always.

One Sunday, when a cold wet sea-haar was drifting in from the Atlantic, so that even the beautiful valley looked like a wretched beggar, a young dark man was brought to Mucklehouse, where I was spending a few days with Archie and Elizabeth Bevan. He was looking for a quiet cottage to compose music in. He was shown a few crofts that could, conceivably, be yet restored. The haar, thickening to a drenching rain, hid the highest cottage in the valley, Bunertoon, that day. Yet there, a year or two later, a fine craftsman David Nelson had the house ready for the composer Peter Maxwell Davies. From Bunertoon – once

'That first glimpse of Rackwick has haunted my imagination
ever since.'

'In Stromness there is now a very beautiful Pier Arts Centre . . .'

the indignant sheep were ousted – proceeded a stream of music known all over the concert halls of the world. Those who listen cannot fail to hear the sounds of Rackwick in the symphonies and songs: Max Davies has woven the sea-wash and bird-calls into his textures with marvellous skill . . . In those first years he dug his own peats and got his water from the spring near the cottage. In storms, he does coastguard duties. He helps Jack Rendall, the one remaining farmer, with the sheep at lambing time.

In Stromness there is now a very beautiful Pier Arts Centre, that once was a merchant's store. Apart from the paintings and sculpture – mostly of the St Ives school, the gift of Margaret Gardiner – there are changing exhibitions; poets and story-tellers read their works there; on the seagirt pier in July reels and strathspeys are played; and it sounds very beautiful with the sea-birds calling around, and the plash of the waves.

The two peaks of the artistic year in Orkney are the Folk Festival in May, when it seems that all the fiddlers and guitarists and folklorists of Scotland come to celebrate, and the islands dance a weekend out.

The St Magnus Festival falls always at midsummer, nowadays for a full week. Now in its eleventh year, it attracts musicians of world-wide renown. On the Saturday evening in 1986 Isaac Stern and the Royal Philharmonic Orchestra gave the world premiere of Peter Maxwell Davies' Violin Concerto in St Magnus Cathedral: the tumult of music-lovers who couldn't get tickets saw the live TV screening in the nearby Arts Theatre... Later the King's Singers performed in a church hall in Kirkwall – Max Davies had arranged four of my Christmas poems in shimmering winter sound. Another group of songs, by an American composer, were settings of poems by Robert Frost. Perhaps it ought to have been noted in the programme that Frost's grandmother came from Hoy. (And, incidentally, Washington Irving's father was a Shapinsay man.)

It seems to me that the arts in Orkney, which flourish so abundantly nowadays, are not a sudden inexplicable accident. True, there were the almost silent centuries between the making of those great medieval ballads, 'The Play of the Lady Odivere' and 'The New Year Song', and the 1920s. But I cannot believe that the arts, in some shape or form, disappeared utterly from the islands. The poems and the tales were oral rather than written down, and most of them have been lost for ever. But the fiddles sang and throbbed on winter nights; the story-teller was never silent; the dance went round and round.

Very deep go the roots. *Orkneyinga Saga* is an anthology of magnificent narrative prose, interrupted here and there by poem and harp-song.

Inside the neolithic tomb of Maeshowe, the Vikings (the 'Jerusalem-farers' of 1154) carved their brief poems in stone, and a dragon and walrus. Some of the mysterious Pictish carvings survive... But Maeshowe itself is a magnificent poem in stone, from thousands of years in the past: an elegy, certainly, for it was a house of the dead. But the stone poets had so arranged the long passage into the tombs, that the setting sun at the winter solstice enters briefly and touches one wall with a golden finger, like a promise of new light and life. Such daring symbolism is rare in modern art and architecture. But it is a part of our heritage, very ancient.

Peter Maxwell Davies rehearsing with Isaac Stern, the world
premiere of his Violin Concerto in St Magnus Cathedral.

# 12
## *Lore*

Why is it that sea water is salt, and the water of burn and well sweet? What are the standing stones – the great circle on the moor and the smaller groups and the individual stones in this field and that? Why are some people ugly, or unlucky all their lives? What are those green mounds and humps here and there in the islands, that look so mysterious on a summer evening late? What are the stars and meteors and planets? Why should certain patterns of sound – music – make the feet want to dance round with the sun? Why does the corn come up green and thick one summer, and sickly the next summer? There is the ruddy ripening sun of June, and the pale wick of December.

Folklore – the stories that a people have cherished over many generations and centuries, and recited again and again across the winter fires – is no collection of idle whimsy, vanities spun to pass the time between supper and bed. They are attempts to come to terms with certain mysterious matters in a people's surroundings and circumstances – to explain things which would otherwise be baffling and therefore hostile. The tales have roots deep in the earliest folk-memory. They might seem to be 'a lot of old bruck and nonsense' to the modern forward-looking number-orientated Orkneyman, but the stories are a part of him whether he likes it or not, and he ignores what Edwin Muir called 'the fable' at his peril. (Science explains the old mysteries, in ever greater detail, but in a cold factual rootless way.)

Here then is why the sea came to be salt. The sea was sweet as the springs and burns when the sea-king captured from the royal palace of Denmark the two giant slave girls Fenia and Menia, along with the mill Grotti which ground out between its ponderous stones whatever you told it to produce: gold or soldiers or roses. Only the huge strength of Fenia and Menia could turn the querns. Somewhere in the North Sea, the prow set fair for the Pentland Firth between Caithness and Orkney, the sea-king ordered Grotti to make salt. The monstrous girls put their shoulders to the stone, and salt gushed out. Probably the sea-king only wanted a little salt to sprinkle on the rib of beef he was eating, but Grotti spewed out salt and laboured to set more hills of salt on the deck of the ship, and frosted the beard of the sea-king. The ship, burdened with salt, teetered and sank in the Pentland Firth, but down below the mill Grotti turns forever. In the Pentland Firth is a whirlpool called The Swelkie: thirled forever to Grotti on the sea bed.

People disappear now and then. If a known person disappears nowadays you inform the police, employ an agency, insert an appeal in a newspaper because, of course, in our common-sense age, there must be some simple factual explanation of the disappearance: the Foreign Legion, the lure of the bright lights of London, simple boredom.

A Rousay girl disappeared long ago. One day, years later, her father and brothers were at sea fishing when a fog came down and shrouded them. They were lost. But soon, through the solid gray and the gray whirls, they sighted land and rowed towards it. They secured their boat and walked up to a house above the shore. They had never been in this island before. The woman of the house took them in and gave them food and drink. The brothers did not know who the woman was, but the father recognised his daughter. She told him that a seal-man had taken her to the vanishing island of Hether Blether, and now she was his wife and quite happy with him and her sea-children . . .

A young man took home to his old parents a strange cold girl. He told them he had fallen in love with her and was going to marry her. The young ones married in the kirk and had children. The old ones died, this winter or that. The hard work of the croft went on, a monotonous necessary cycle of labour, year after year. The croft-wife made cheese and bannocks and butter, rocked the cradle, looked to the hearth-fire, kept the water buckets brimming. Then one day she went away as suddenly as she had come. She was never seen again. Her deserted man, when he looked one day among his barn rafters, saw that the seal-pelt he kept there had vanished – the skin he had taken from a rock the very night he led home to his parents the girl whose vowels when she spoke were cold sea sounds.

The standing stones are sun-stricken giants. Orkney was full of giants in those days, violent argumentative monsters. The earth shook when they moved. They hurled vast rocks at each other. Cubbie Roo was a giant in the island of Wyre. Mothers in the last century would warn their ill-answering children: 'Cubbie Roo'll get thee!' But in fact Cubbie Roo is a folk-version of an actual historical figure, Kolbein Hruga the laird of Wyre in Norse times. Kolbein Hruga must have been a formidable man indeed, so to be invested with the huge girth and trappings of legend.

A giant who lived in Scotland decided to build a new house. He came to Orkney to get stones and earth. With three vast steps he splashed his way across the Pentland Firth. He scooped two fistfuls of earth from the Mainland and put them in the cubbie (straw basket) that he carried on his shoulder. He turned for home. Some of the soil spilled from his basket into the sea. Another step, and the basket-strap broke: all the earth fell into the sea with an almighty splash! The two grooves in the Mainland soon filled with water from burns and underground springs; they became the Loch of Stenness and the Loch of Harray. The first soil spilling from the giant's cubbie became the little green island of Graemsay; the second dollop became Hoy with its dark hills and cliffs.

Trows lived in the green mounds or howes that occur everywhere in the islands. Often they were evil beings who did mischief to croft and croft folk. Even today, if a person has been sick for a time, he is said to be 'trowie' – that is, the trows have smitten him. The trows sought always to exchange their own ugly deformed offspring for human children, and sometimes they succeeded; and that is the reason why some folk are uglier, awkwarder, more misshapen than others. At midwinter the trows were especially active; reading the old accounts one has the impression that every little isolated bewintered croft was sieged, between sunset and dawn, by dark malevolent hordes. Special words had to be uttered over the farm-implements, ploughs and querns. All actions had to be performed sun-wise: withershins was the way of witch and trow. Lintel and bed had to be 'sained', at first with a cross, and later with a bible: the trows had no power over those holy symbols.

113

Stones of Stenness: 'The standing stones are sun-stricken giants.'

But possibly there were good helpful under-earth creatures too: they kept the wells pure and sweet, they sent up the corn into the ripening sun and rain and wind. They didn't, of course, do these kindnesses for nothing. What they loved most about human beings were the patterns they made, especially their sound-patterns: music. So they would linger, drunk with reels, at every barn door where there was a wedding reception or a harvest home.

The strangest of all the old legends concerns the two fiddlers returning home late on a summer night from a country wedding. The road led them past a cluster of those green 'knowes' which were known to be the dwelling-places of trows. The young fiddlers, perhaps a little drunk with the wedding ale, conversed with each other, their voices loud and high in the glimmering summer stillness. Suddenly one of the fiddlers became aware that he was getting no answers; he turned; his friend was not there. Then fiddle music flashed out from the heart of the knowe. The solitary fiddler ran home in terror, clutching his varnished silent bird to his breast... Years later this same fiddler, with wrinkles at the eyes and ash in his beard now, was walking along the same road on a summer midnight when he became aware of a strange but familiar footstep beside him. He turned; he recognised with a pang the fiddler who had disappeared so long ago. The young man had aged not a single hour; he had the apples in his face and his beard was untarnished gold.

The mind delights to linger on this beautiful story. Under the surface pattern, the old story-teller seems to be speculating on the nature of art: what we mean when we say that, at its best, all creative art is 'timeless'. In their chamber under the hill the trows had asked the stolen fiddler – after he had tasted their delicious meat and drink – to play one tune for them; then they would let him go. After what seemed ten minutes or so the fiddler was out under the summer stars again. But in fact twenty-five harvests had been sown and reaped (or ten harvests, or a hundred, according to different versions).

> *'Darst thu gang b' the black furrow*
> *This night, thee and thy song?...'*
> *'Weet me mooth wi' the Lenten ale,*
> *I'll go along.'*
>
> *They spied him near the black furrow*
> *B' the glim o' the wolf star.*

*Slow the dance was in his feet,*
*Dark the fiddle he bore ...*

*There stood three men at the black furrow*
*And one was clad in green.*
*They've taen the fiddler b' the hand*
*Where he was no more seen ...*

*They've put the gowd cup in his hand,*
*Elfin bread on his tongue.*
*There he bade a hundred years*
*Him and his lawless song ...*

Perhaps indeed fertility is the root of the story. Was it in a summertime of poor corn that the fiddler was dragged down into the earth? Was his song meant to purify choked and polluted sources? The old story-teller may well have been upholding the dignity of all those who 'make things beautiful and good'. A tale or a statue or a song is not made to give a moment's fleeting pleasure to superior cultured minds; they are absolutely necessary for the well-being and health of a community. Without good art – vision – a people perishes.

*Art must be of use – a coercive rhyme, to strand a whale on the rock, a scratch on stone to make the corn grow. What are all those fiddles and statues and books for? ...*

# 13
# *A Nature Anthology*

There is such a great wealth of books, over the last century or so, on the natural history of Orkney, in all its aspects, that any précis would be the barest skeleton. (To write an essay on the subject would only reveal this writer's profound ignorance.) What might be of interest is to discover man's changing relationship with his environment and fellow-creatures over the centuries from Jo Ben's giants and monsters and miracles of the sixteenth century, through the benign eye that Rev. James Wallace turned on nature a century and a half later, to Rev. George Barry's huge scientific catalogue of 1805, which yet contains much fresh and delightfully-phrased observation. I hope that this approach to the subject will add another dimension to the book: to look at Orkney through contemporary eyes alone amounts, in a way, to distortion, for other times have seen it quiet differently, and there is nothing like the prose of another age to bring that time to full and vivid life. Most of Jo Ben's monsters have vanished; so, alas, have some of the birds mentioned by Wallace and Barry. But most remain.

Hardly a thing is known about Jo Ben. The name itself is strange – possibly a contracted form of John Bellenden. The tradition is that he was an ecclesiastic of some kind.

It seems unlikely that he visited every island; at any rate, some are given much fuller treatment than others.

*North Ronaldsay* In the north part of the island large native animals (selchies) are captured in nets made of hemp, and there is also there a large rock, called Selchskerry, where sea fowl live and nest... The people of the island interchanging grumbles among themselves at delays coming in the way, approach the rock with large hazel sticks. At first the animals, eyeing them with anger and gnashing of teeth, strive to move away with wide open mouths: then they attack with all their strength... If the first beast escapes without injury, all the others attack the men with their teeth, but if the first fall and die, all the others take to flight and are easily captured...

*Sanday* English and German vessels often meet with destruction in one part of the island, towards the east, called the Har of Lopness. I myself, passing through this island, being fatigued, rested myself at a church called the Holy Cross, and in the churchyard saw innumerable skulls of men, about a thousand, larger than the heads of any living tribe (or larger than three heads of those now living), and I extracted teeth from the gums of the size of a hazel nut... Rabbits are abundant in summer, and in winter are so tame that they are taken into houses...

*Stronsay* A great monster, called Troicis, often associates with women living here. When I resided there a beautiful woman that was married to an able-bodied farmer, was much tormented by a great spirit and both were seen, against the husband's will, lying on one bed. The woman at last became emaciated with sorrow. I advised that she might get freedom by prayer, almsgiving, and fasting: the duration of her trouble lasted a year. The description of the monster is this: he was covered with seaweed over his whole body, and resembled a dark horse with wrinkled skin, with limbs like a horse.

*Auskerry* Another uncultivated island, where the horses are very ferocious.

*Faray* The meaning of the name is the beautiful or pleasant isle. It is very suitable for animals, especially cows, which there graze on bushes with great satisfaction, and the boys sing to the dull beasts. The whole island is plentiful of corn and fishes.

*Eynhallow* It is of old times related that here, if the standing corn be cut down after the setting of the sun, unexpectedly there is a flowing of blood from the stalks of the grain; also it is said that if a horse is fastened after sundown, it will easily get loose.

*Eday* There is a great abundance of cattle. The men sometimes fight with great monsters, which they cut up in dregs (or melt the dregs into fat), then boil and cook into oil.

*Damsay* No frogs, toads, or other noxious terrestrial creatures are found here. The women here are sterile, and if they do become pregnant never bring forth with life.

*Deerness* This parish of old times was wooded and many wild beasts were found here: at length, floods coming, the trees were uprooted and were submerged.

*St Olai* The women here are given to excess in luxuries and pleasures; this is supposed to be caused by the abundance of fish obtainable. Here is a very high mountain named Whitford.

*Stenhouse* In this parish there is a large lake, 24 miles in circuit. On a little hill near the lake in a tomb was found the bones of a man in length 14 feet, and money was found under the head of the dead man.

*Stromness* Beneficial winds here blow called Etesian for about forty days every year about the dog days. Here is a very dangerous bridge for travellers, called the Bridge of Vaith, where many perish.

*Pomona* All the men are very drunken and wanton, and fight among themselves. For an example of their friendship, if one neighbour invites another and if the invited before his departure has not vomited he assails his host and there is much strife . . .

Jo Ben, if he was a wandering friar, lingered still in the dim region between fantasy and nature. The Rev. James Wallace saw wonders everywhere too, but the wonders he contemplated and wrote about are in the order of nature. It can be inferred, too, that he was a kindlier man than Jo Ben; it would have been pleasant to sit with him in his rectory at Sanday and (later) Kirkwall, and share a bowl of hot punch with him on a winter evening. He flourished when the tides of religious establishment in Scotland fluctuated between Episcopalianism and Presbyterianism. He himself was a bishop's man, but nothing of the rage of the period stains his serene pages.

*A Stone from the Clouds*  The Air and Clouds here, by the Operation of the Sun, do sometime generate several things, for Instance some few years hence some Fishermen Fishing half a League from land, over against *Copinsha*, in a fair Day there fell down from the Air a Stone about the bigness of a Football, which fell in the midst of the Boat, and Sprung a Lake in it, to the great hazard of the lives of the men that were in it, which could be no other but some substance generated in the Clouds. The Stone was like condensed or Petrified Clay . . .

*Ice in Summer*  Sometimes the Rains descend not by drops but by Spouts of Water, as if whole Clouds fell down at once. About Four years ago, after a greater thunder in the Moneth of *June*, there fell a great Flake of Ice, more than a Foot thick.

*The Teeming Earth*  This Countrey abounds with variety both of Field and Garden Plants, Especially Cabbage, Turnipe, Parsnipe, Carrot, Crummock, Artichock, grow to a greater bigness here than I have seen them else where. I have seen Strawberries that would be three inch about, sometimes the Herbs are monstrously fruitful, for out of the flower of a Marigold, I have seen twelve more growing; the like I have seen in the wild Deasie . . .

*Sheepdead*  The Sheep usually die of a Disease called the *Sheepdead*, which is occasioned by great quantities of little Animals like to Flouks of an inch long, which are engendered in the Liver. I put one of them in a Microscope, and found it like a little Flouk wanting finns.

*Horses, Swine, Rabbits, Snails*  The Horses are but little, Yet strong and well mettald, most of which they get from *Zetland*, and are called *Shelties*. There are great herds of Swine, and rich cuningars almost in every Isle, well stored with Rabbets . . . There is a great Snail that hath a bright white stone growing in it.

*Trees* There is no Forrest or Wood in all this Country, nor any Trees, except some that are in the Bishop's Garden at *Kirkwall*, where are some Ashes and thorn and Plum-Trees... Yet it seems there hath been Woods growing in this Country, for in the Mosses they find Trees with their Branches intire of 20 or 30 foot length.

*Waters* This Countrey being divided in small Islands, it cannot be expected there should be in it any Rivers, yet there is every where a great many Bourns and torrents, well replenished with Trouts, both small and great, some of them like to young Salmon.

There is a large Loch in the *Mainland*, called the Loch of *Stennis*, but unfruitful... The Loch of *Swanna* in the *Mainland*, will have in some parts a thick scumm of Copper Colour upon it, which makes some think there is some Mine under it.

Nothing much is known either about Dr George Barry, minister of Shapinsay. In 1805 he published in Edinburgh his massive *The History of the Orkney Islands: in which is comprehended an Account of their Present as well as their Ancient State; together with The Advantages they Possess for Several Branches of Industry, and the Means by which they may be Improved. Illustrated With an Accurate and Extensive Map of the Whole Islands, and With Plates of some of the most Interesting Objects they contain.*

Wallace's attempt to see Orkney as a whole is a frail web compared to the massive monument erected by the scholarship of Barry; in little more than a century so much more information had accumulated. Barry was one of a scholarly group of Orkney Presbyterian ministers which included Rev. George Low (Birsay) and Dr Charles Clouston (Sandwick).

The century of reason had intervened between Wallace and Barry; some of the wonder has gone, but still Barry writes about the flora and fauna of the islands with charm and fluency, and with the exactitude and authority of the new science. Of his long catalogue there is space to quote only a very brief selection.

*A Lead Mine* Near the manse of Stromness, which is about a mile to the westward of the town, there may be seen, embedded in a rock consisting of schistose clay, Lydian stone, which it contains in its cavities filled with bitumen;

and, on the adjacent shore, in a rock immediate between schistose and indurated clay, many pieces of galena.

Struck with the flattering appearance of these, men of skill in mineralogy were induced to inspect the place with accuracy; and as they judged it probable that lead might be found there in abundance, a company of miners were employed, who wrought for some time, but were at length compelled to desist, being convinced that all the metal which they could procure, would not be adequate to the expence of the labour.

*The Garden* In the flower-garden, the rose, the tulip, the carnation, the pink, the primrose, with a multitude of other flowers, are cultivated with success; while the kitchen garden produces cabbage, broccoli, cauliflower, peas, beans, spinach, onions, leeks, parsley, cresses, beets, lettuces, turnips, carrots, parsnips, celery, and artichokes; all of which are good of their kind, but particularly the last is of unrivalled excellence.

The fruit garden, though it produces in abundance, excellent black, white, and red currants, is very inferior in the apples, pears, plums, cherries, gooseberries, and strawberries that it produces, in respect both to size and flavour.

*The Lobster, (Cancer grammarus, Lin. syst. Nat.)* on account of its superior excellence, is justly entitled to the first place in the lowest order. Around almost all our rocky shores, these fishes are caught in the summer months, in a depth of water from two to six fathoms, during the night commonly, or, if in the day, only in dark weather. The nets made use of for this purpose are in the form of bags, fixed to iron hoops of about two feet and a half diameter, with pieces of lead to sink them, baited with fish, flesh, or garbage of any kind, which the lobsters devour with the utmost avidity. As soon as they are caught, their claws are bound with twine, to prevent their maiming or killing each other; and they are put into large chests, which are anchored in the water in bays or harbours, where they lye unmolested, till put on board the smacks that carry them, in their wells, alive, weekly, in thousands, to the London market.

*Herring, (Clupea harengus)* in the months of July and August, not only pay an annual visit to our coasts, as might have been expected from our situation in the track of the great northern shoal, but enter into and continue for some time in our bays, creeks, and friths; and depart unmolested; as we are either destitute of time, capital, or industry, to avail ourselves of this inexhaustible treasure.

*The Coalfish, (Gadus carbonarius)* which is so well known here by the name of the *sellock*, *cuth*, or *seth*, according as the age of it is either one two or more years, is much more abundant than any other, and, indeed, excels in number almost all the rest of our fish taken together. The fry of this species appear first in May, when they are small in size, and few in number. In August, they increase considerably in both respects; but towards winter, when the seas begin to be stormy, they rush into, and often occupy, most of our bays, in which they are caught in myriads, for their livers, which furnish oil for the lamps, and their fish, that constitutes an extensive and valuable article of food to the poor people.

*The Toad, (Rana bufo)* is sometimes seen in the evenings in gardens, and such-like places, crawling but never leaping, as the frog does; and is of an appearance, which, to most people, is not only ugly in the extreme, but even frightful and disgusting. Hence perhaps the opinion that has very generally prevailed, that this reptile is pernicious, and has either by its bite, its saliva, or some other means, sometimes transfused its poison into man, as well as other animals. But this opinion is neither supported by the structure of the animal, as it appears on dissection, nor yet by the instances that are adduced . . .

*The Gannet, (Pelecanus baffanus)* which has here got the name of the *Solan*, or *Solandgoose*, frequents our bays, and fishes in a very peculiar manner. The birds of this species do not breed here; but many of them do on the Stack of Suliskerry, a holm or uninhabited island, a little to the south-west of this country.

*The Common Gull, (Larus canus)* our *sea-maw*, or *white-maw*, is so numerous on all our shores, rocks, bays, and harbours, that their noise is sometimes disagreeable.

*The Auk, (Alka torda)* the same with our *baukie*, comes hither in March, and without delay takes possession of almost all the high rocks on the headlands, where it lays only one large egg in the shelve of a bare rock, exposed to the heat of the sun, which probably assists in hatching it.

The gannets on Stack Skerry, 40 miles west of Orkney's Mainland.

*The Sky-Lark, (Alauda arvensis)* remains with us constantly; it begins to sing about the first of February, and continues its pleasant notes for the most part of summer.

*The Kestrel, (Falco tinnunculus)* which, from its motion in the air, we name the *windcuffer*, may frequently be observed, as if stationed with its eyes fixed on the ground, to discover its prey, small birds, mice, and chickens, on which it darts down with such unerring speed, that they very seldom escape its talons.

*The Ringtail Eagle, (Falco fulvus)* which, together with the other eagles, is here named the *erne*, is very frequently seen on the hills, builds on the rocks, is of a large size, distinguished from the rest by a band of white encompassing the root of the tail, and the legs being covered with feathers down to the very feet; and is of such prodigious strength, that it is sometimes said to have carried from a considerable distance to its eyry not only fowls, but lambs, pigs, and even, in some instances, young children, if we trust the authority of a respectable author, whose account is also supported by tradition . . .

*The Otter, (Mustela lutra)* is very frequently found burrowing on the shores of the sea, and on the banks of fresh-water lochs, where it lives on cod-fish, conger-eels, and all kinds of trout. It is so nice in its taste, as only to consume the finer parts, while it leaves the remainder. The fur, which is excellent, is the only thing valuable, and, if the animal be killed in winter, sells for about ten shillings Sterling.

*The Seal, (Phoca vitulina)* which is here generally known by the name of *selchy*, is very common on most of our low shores, but particularly on those of the small holms and remote skerries, where it is frequently seen reposing and basking in the sun, in fine calm weather, and where it brings forth its young. The species in this place is very numerous; and some of them are so large as to measure eight or nine feet from the point of the nose to the claws of the hind legs; and, at the shoulders, they are nearly as much in circumference. If boats be passing near their haunts, they seem to discover some curiosity in looking steadfastly, and listening to the stroke of the oars, the conversation of the people, or to any noise that is unusual.

Ewe and lamb feeding on seaweed, North Ronaldsay.

They are valuable for their skins, (of which shoes slippers, and covers for trunks and saddles are made), and for the oil which they furnish. In order to obtain these very useful articles, the animals are knocked down with clubs, caught in nets, and shot with muskets ... In some few places, the flesh of the young seals is used fresh; and both in that state and that of hams, is said to be tolerable.

*The Dog, (Canis familiaris)* here is not remarkable, for the only ones we have, are the greyhound, kept for catching rabbits; the land and water spaniel and the pointer, used for the purpose of carrying and fowling; the mastiff, for guarding ships, and protecting houses; the terrier, used formerly for searching out rabbits; some varieties of the lapdog; and the shepherd's dog, with its mongrels. This faithful animal is the constant guardian of the corn and the grass in the fields, as well as of the production of the gardens, against the whole tribe of domestic granivorous animals. To a little farmer, in a mean condition, his dog is of even more value than a horse or a cow; since it is by his means alone that he can preserve the produce of his possession.

*The Sheep, (Ovis aries)* here is a peculiar breed, and, from some features in its character, seems to have sprung from the same stock with those of Iceland, the Ferroes, and Shetland. Though of a tolerably good kind, and everywhere very numerous, they are of little benefit to the owners, owing to the absurd custom of suffering them to run wild on the extensive commons, exposed to the violence of the sea, the severity of the weather, the depredation of various distempers, and to the dogs and eagles ... In some places, the sheep wander to the shore at low-water, and make a plentiful meal of the different kinds of sea-weed; and when they have been accustomed to live much on that food, their flesh is of a dark colour, dry, and of a coarse texture; and, when prepared for the table, has been thought to bear some resemblance to venison ...

# For further reading

Bailey, Patrick, *Orkney* (Newton Abbot: David & Charles, 1971)

Balfour, E., *Orkney Birds*, Status and Guide (Stromness: C. Senior, 1972)

Brown, George Mackay, *The Golden Bird* (London: John Murray, 1987)

– *Selected Poems* (London: The Hogarth Press, 1977)

Brown, Malcolm and Meehan, Patricia, *Scapa Flow* (London: Allen Lane, 1968)

Defoe, Daniel, *The Pirate Gow* (Edinburgh: Gordon Wright, reissued 1978)

Ferguson, David, *The Wrecks of Scapa Flow* (Orkney: The Orkney Press, 1985)

Firth, John, *Reminiscences of an Orkney Parish* (Stromness: Orkney Natural History Society, reissued 1974)

Linklater, Eric, *Fanfare for a Tin Hat* (London: Macmillan, 1970)

– *White-Maa's Saga* (London: Jonathan Cape, 1929)

Marwick, Ernest W., *The Folklore of Orkney and Shetland* (London: Batsford, 1975)

Marwick, Hugh, *Orkney Farm Names* (Kirkwall: W. R. Mackintosh, 1952)

Miller, Ronald, *Orkney* (London: Batsford, 1976)

Muir, Edwin, *An Autobiography* (London: The Hogarth Press, reissued 1987)

– *Collected Poems* (London: Faber & Faber, 1952)

*The New Orkney Book*, ed. by J. Shearer (London: Nelson, 1966)

*Orkneyinga Saga*, trans. by Hermann Pálsson and Paul Edwards (London: Penguin Books, 1978)

Rendall, Robert, *Country Sonnets and Other Poems* (Kirkwall: Orcadian, n.d.)

– *The Hidden Land* (Kirkwall: Kirkwall Press, 1966)

– *Orkney Variants and Other Poems* (Kirkwall: Kirkwall Press, n.d.)

– *Shore Poems and Other Verse* (Kirkwall: Kirkwall Press, 1957)

Renfrew, Colin, *Investigations in Orkney* (London: Thames & Hudson, 1979)

Skea, Bessie, *A Countrywoman's Diary* (Edinburgh: Gordon Wright, 1983)

Thomson, William P. L., *A History of Orkney* (Edinburgh: The Mercat Press, 1987)

Troup, J. A. and Eunson, F., *Stromness: 150 Years a Burgh, 1817–1967* (Stromness: W. R. Rendall, 1967)